family circle

PIES
sweet & savoury

The Family Circle® Promise of Success

Welcome to the world of Confident Cooking,
created for you in the Australian **Family Circle®
Test Kitchen,** where recipes are double-tested by
our team of home economists to achieve a
high standard of success—and delicious
results every time.

MURDOCH
BOOKS

TEST KITCHEN PERFECTION

You'll never make a wrong move with a Family Circle® step-by-step cookbook. Our team of home economists has tested and refined the recipes so that you can create fabulous food in your own kitchen. Follow our easy instructions and step-by-step photographs and you'll feel like there is a master chef in the kitchen guiding you every step of the way.

All recipes are double-tested by our team of home economists. When we test our recipes, we rate them for ease of preparation. The following cookery ratings are on the recipes in this book, making them easy to use and understand.

A single Cooking with Confidence symbol indicates a recipe that is simple and generally quick to make—perfect for beginners.

Two symbols indicate the need for just a little more care and a little more time.

Three symbols indicate special dishes that need more investment in time, care and patience—but the results are worth it.

The Publisher thanks: Chief Australia; Breville Holdings Pty Ltd; Kambrook; Bertolli Olive Oil; Southcorp Appliances; Sheldon & Hammond.
Front cover: Plum pie, page 109
Inside front cover: Chicken, leek and mushroom pies, page 12
Back cover: Cocktail leek pies, page 38

CONTENTS

Top: Beef, stout and potato pie, page 27   ***Bottom left:*** *Mini spinach pies, page 18*   ***Bottom right:*** *Chocolate fudge pecan pie, page 82*

Perfect pies every time

A crunchy pastry enclosing a mouth-watering filling is a delight. However, some people miss out on the joy of a home-made pie because of their fear of making pastry. We want to guide you through pastry making and show you how easy it is. Most of the pies in this book use a simple shortcrust pastry, and once you have made it yourself, you will discover how superior it is to bought pastry.

WHICH PASTRY?

For most of our pie recipes, you can make your own pastry or buy a ready-made one. If we specify a home-made pastry it is because the taste is better with that particular pie.

We have used only a few types of pastry so once you master them you will be able to make any of the pies with confidence. To begin with, choose the easiest pastries such as shortcrust or quick flaky. Apart from butter pastries, some pies use olive oil and others lard. Some shortcrusts have sugar or an egg added, and for these you can use a bought shortcrust, but the pastry won't be quite as rich. Normal shortcrust can be used for sweet pies but sweet pastry is most commonly used. You will need 375 g to line a 23 cm pie dish.

INGREDIENTS

Pastry at its simplest is a mixture of flour with half its weight in some form of fat and bound with water.
Flour Plain white flour is the one most commonly used for pastry. For a slightly different texture, a combination of wholemeal plain and plain white flour is used. Store flour in an airtight container.
Fat Butter is the most commonly used fat for making pastry and imparts a wonderful colour to the pastry. Use real butter, not margarine or softened butter blends. Sometimes a mixture of butter and lard is used, sometimes all lard. Lard gives a lovely flaky texture. Butter and lard are usually chilled and cut into cubes to make it easier to incorporate them into the flour, keeping the pastry

cooler and more manageable. Generally, unsalted butter should be used for sweet pastries and salted butter for savoury pies. Olive oil is used for some pies, such as spinach pie, for a different texture.
Salt is added to both sweet and savoury pastry to add flavour.
Sugar Caster sugar is used in making sweet shortcrust pastry as its fine texture ensures that it blends well.
Liquid The usual binding liquid is iced water, but sometimes an egg or an egg yolk will be used to enrich the pastry. You will find that most pastry recipes only give an approximate liquid measure because it varies according to the flour, the temperature, the altitude and the humidity. Add a little at a time and work it in until the pastry achieves the desired result.

TOOLS OF THE TRADE

A few tools that are specifically designed to assist in the making of pastry are a worthwhile investment. However, as you can see below, it is possible to adapt things you already have in your kitchen and still make a successful pastry.

Marble pastry board Although not strictly necessary, marble boards are favoured by pastry makers for their cool and hygienic surface. If you don't have one, you can sit a roasting tin full of iced water on your work surface for a while to cool the surface before rolling your pastry.

Rolling pins are an essential tool in pastry making. Many varieties are available, from traditional wooden ones to marble, plastic and stainless steel. Lightly sprinkle your rolling pin with flour. You can use an empty glass bottle, but it is much harder to roll.

Pastry brushes are used for glazing. A glaze gives the cooked pastry a lovely crispness and colour. Pastry can also be sealed and joined by brushing the edges or borders with milk or beaten egg. Use only a small amount of liquid, otherwise the pastry will become soggy.

Baking beads Reusable baking beads are used to weigh down pastry during blind baking. They are available in kitchenware shops and department stores. Dried beans or uncooked rice can also be used and reused.

Cutters are available in all shapes and sizes. They are used to cut out bases and tops for small individual pies and to cut out pieces of dough to decorate the pie. Cutters may need to be dusted lightly with flour to prevent them from sticking to the pastry. If you don't have a pastry cutter, a fine-rimmed glass, turned upside-down, is a good substitute.

Pie tins and dishes are available in myriad styles. While testing the pies for this book we baked in metal, glass and ceramic pie dishes. The best bottom crusts were achieved when we baked in metal pie tins.

Baking paper is very useful when rolling out pastry. The dough is rolled out between two sheets, the top sheet is removed and the pastry is inverted into the tin before removing the other sheet. Baking paper is also used to line pastry shells when blind baking.

Food processor While not essential, a food processor can make pastry-making much easier. As pastry should be kept cool, a processor helps greatly as you don't have to touch the dough as you combine the ingredients. The food processor method is described on page 7. If you prefer, you can use the processor just to combine the butter and flour before continuing mixing by hand.

PASTRY BASICS

The following hints will help ensure a successful pastry:

■ Work in a cool kitchen in cool weather if possible. If you are cooking in the middle of summer, air conditioning or a fan can help.

■ Make sure all the ingredients are as cool as possible and that they stay cool during the preparation.

■ Because your hands are warm, it is important to handle the pastry as little as possible. Cool your hands by running them under cold water.

■ Work quickly to ensure the pastry stays cool. Over-handling will toughen and shrink cooked pastry.

■ Flours vary in their moisture content. As well, the temperature, humidity and altitude can affect the moisture content. Because of this unpredictability, the amount of liquid added to pastry dough varies and it is not added all at once. Test the dough by pinching a little piece together. If it holds together and doesn't crumble, you won't need more liquid. If the pastry is too dry, it will be difficult to put into tins; if too wet it will shrink when cooked.

■ Pastry should be wrapped in plastic and refrigerated for 20–30 minutes before rolling or shaping. If the weather is hot, refrigerate the pastry for at least 30 minutes.

■ For ease of rolling, roll out the pastry between sheets of baking paper.

■ Pies with a bottom crust benefit from being cooked on a heated metal baking tray, so put the tray in the oven as the oven warms up. When the oven is at the correct temperature, place your tin or pie dish on the tray.

■ Pastry can be stored in the refrigerator for two days or it can be frozen for up to three months. Ensure that it is well sealed in plastic wrap and clearly labelled and dated. Thaw on a wire rack. This allows air to circulate around the pastry.

■ Pastry should always be cooked in a preheated oven, never one that has not yet reached the specified temperature. It is a good idea to use an oven thermometer.

■ Pies can be successfully frozen as long as the filling is suitable (don't freeze creamy, egg fillings) and the pastry has not already been frozen. For best results, a frozen pie should be reheated in a slow oven.

■ To test whether a pie is cooked through, insert a metal skewer into the centre. If the skewer is cold, the pie needs to cook a little longer.

SHORTCRUST PASTRY

This recipe makes about 375 g of basic shortcrust pastry, which is enough to line the base of a 23 cm pie dish, or just the top. If you need to use 750 g of pastry, simply use double the quantity.

To make 375 g of basic shortcrust pastry, you will need 2 cups (250 g) plain flour, 125 g chilled butter, chopped into small pieces, and 2–3 tablespoons iced water. If you want to line the top and base, you will need 600 g and for this you need 400 g plain flour, 180 g chilled butter, chopped into small pieces, and 3–4 tablespoons iced water.

1 Remove the butter from the fridge 20 minutes before you make the pastry, except in hot weather. Sift the flour and 1/4 teaspoon of salt into a large bowl. Sifting the flour will aerate the dough and help make the finished pastry crisp and light.

2 Add the chopped butter and rub it into the flour with your fingertips (not your palms as they tend to be too warm) until the mixture resembles fine breadcrumbs. As you rub the butter into the flour, lift it up high and let it fall back into the bowl. If applicable, stir in other dry ingredients such as sugar or herbs.

3 Make a well in the centre, add nearly all the water and mix with a flat-bladed knife, using a cutting rather than a stirring action, turning the bowl with your free hand. The mixture will come together in small beads of dough. If necessary, add more water, a teaspoon at a time, until the dough comes together. Test the dough by pinching a little piece between your fingers. If it doesn't

Making shortcrust pastry

Add the chopped butter to the flour and rub it in until it resembles fine crumbs.

Mix in the water with a knife, using a cutting, rather than a stirring, action.

Roll out the pastry, from the centre outwards, rotating the dough.

hold together, it needs more water. If the pastry is too dry it will fall apart when you roll it and, if too wet, it will be sticky and shrink when baked.

4 Gather the dough together and lift out onto a lightly floured work surface or a sheet of baking paper. Press the dough together into a ball. The trick here is not to knead or handle the dough too much, but just to press it together and then flatten it slightly into a disc. Refrigerate in plastic wrap or a plastic bag for at least 20–30 minutes—this makes it easier to roll and helps prevent shrinkage during cooking. If the weather is hot, refrigerate for at least 30 minutes.

5 Roll out the pastry between two sheets of baking paper or plastic wrap, or on a lightly floured surface. Always roll from the centre outwards, rotating the dough, rather than backwards and forwards.

6 If you used baking paper to roll out the pastry, remove the top sheet, carefully invert the pastry over the tin, making sure you centre the pastry, as it can't be moved once in place, and then peel away the paper. If you rolled out on a floured surface, roll the pastry back over the rolling pin so it is hanging, then ease it into the tin.

7 Once the pastry is in the tin, quickly lift up the sides so they don't break over the edges of the tin, which can be sharp. Use a small ball of excess dough to help ease and press the pastry shell into the side of the tin. Allow the excess to hang over the side and, if using a flan tin, roll the rolling pin over the top of the tin to cut off the excess pastry. If you are using a glass or ceramic pie dish, use a small sharp knife to cut away the excess pastry.

8 However gently you handle dough, it is bound to shrink a little, so let it sit slightly above the sides of the tin. If you rolled off the excess pastry with a rolling pin, you may find it has bunched down the sides. Gently press the sides of the pastry with your thumbs to flatten and lift it. Refrigerate in the tin for 15 minutes to relax it and prevent or minimise shrinkage. Preheat the oven.

Shortcrust variations

RICH SHORTCRUST PASTRY

This is often used for fruit pies, flans and tarts as it gives a richer, crisper crust. To transform a basic shortcrust into a rich one, gradually add a beaten egg yolk to the flour with 2–3 tablespoons iced water as above in step 3. Mix with a flat-bladed knife as described.

SWEET SHORTCRUST PASTRY

Follow the directions for the rich shortcrust and add 2 tablespoons caster or icing sugar after the butter has been rubbed into the flour. Proceed as outlined above.

FLAVOUR VARIATIONS

Herb pastry: Add 2–3 tablespoons chopped fresh herbs to the flour.
Cheese pastry: Add 60 g grated Parmesan to the flour.
Seed pastry: Add 2 teaspoons sesame or poppy seeds to the flour.
Mustard pastry: Add 1–2 tablespoons wholegrain mustard to the flour.
Nut pastry: Add 2–3 tablespoons ground nuts, such as almonds, walnuts or pecans, to the flour.
Citrus pastry: Add 2–3 teaspoons finely chopped orange or lemon zest to the flour.
English shortcrust pastry: Use half butter and half lard, and proceed as described above. Lard gives the pastry a good flavour and texture.

Food processor shortcrust

Shortcrust pastry can be made quickly and successfully with a food processor. The obvious advantage of using a food processor is its speed but, as well as this, you don't handle the pastry much so it stays cool. Process the flour and cold chopped butter in short bursts, using the pulse button if your machine has one, until the mixture resembles fine breadcrumbs. While the processor is running, add a teaspoon of water at a time until the dough holds together. Process in short bursts again and don't over-process or the pastry will toughen and shrink while cooking. You will know you have overworked the pastry if it forms into a ball in the processor. It should just come together in clumps. Gather it into a ball on a lightly floured surface, flatten it into a disc and wrap in plastic wrap, then refrigerate it for 20–30 minutes.

PUFF PASTRY

This is made by layering dough with butter and folding and rolling to create hundreds of layers. When baked, the butter melts and the dough produces steam, forcing the layers apart and making the pastry rise. The pastry should be chilled for at least 30 minutes before baking, to relax it.

For perfect puff pastry which rises evenly, the edges must be cut cleanly with a sharp knife or cutter, not torn. Egg glazes give a shine but must be applied carefully—any drips down the side may glue the layers together and stop them rising evenly.

Always bake puff pastry at a very high temperature—it should rise evenly, so if your oven has areas of uneven heat, turn the pastry around when it has set. When cooked, the top and base should be brown, with only a small amount of under-baked dough inside, and the layers should be visible.

Puff pastry is not always perfect—it may fall over or not rise to quite the heights you had imagined—but provided you don't burn it, and it is well cooked, it will still be delicious.

The recipe we have given below makes about 500 g of puff pastry. You will notice that we've given a range for the butter quantity. If you've never made puff pastry before, you'll find it easier to use the lower amount. You will need 200–250 g unsalted butter, 2 cups (250 g) plain flour, 1/2 teaspoon salt and 2/3 cup (170 ml) iced water.

1 Melt 30 g butter in a saucepan. Sift the flour and salt onto a work surface and make a well in the centre. Pour the melted butter and water into the well and blend with your fingertips, gradually drawing in the flour. You should end up with a crumb mixture. If it seems a little dry, add a few extra drops of water before bringing it all together to form a dough.
2 Cut the dough with a pastry scraper, using a downward cutting action, then turn the dough and repeat in the opposite direction. The dough should now come together to

form a soft ball. Score a cross in the top to prevent shrinkage and refrigerate in plastic wrap for 15–20 minutes.
3 Soften the remaining butter by pounding it between two sheets of baking paper with a rolling pin. Then, still between the sheets of baking paper, roll it into a 10 cm square. The butter must be the same consistency as the dough or they will not roll out the same amount and the layers will not be even. If the butter is too soft it will squeeze out of the sides, and if it is too hard it will break through the dough and disturb the layers.
4 Put the pastry on a well-floured surface. Roll it out to form a cross, leaving the centre slightly thicker than the arms. Place the butter in the centre of the cross and fold over each of the arms to make a parcel. Tap and roll out the dough to form a 15 x 45 cm rectangle. Make this as neat as possible, squaring off the corners—otherwise, every time you fold, the edges will become less neat and the layers will not be even.
5 Fold the dough like a letter, the top third down and the bottom third up, brushing off any excess flour between the layers. Give the dough a quarter turn to your left and press the seam sides down with the rolling pin to seal them. Re-roll and fold as before to complete two turns and mark the dough by gently pressing into the corner with your fingertip for each turn—this will remind you where you're up to. Wrap the dough in plastic wrap and chill again for at least 30 minutes.
6 Re-roll and fold the pastry twice more and then chill, then roll again to complete six turns. If it is a very hot day, you may need to chill for 30 minutes after each turn, rather than doing a double turn as described above. The pastry should now be an even yellow and is ready to use—if it looks a little streaky, roll and fold once more. The aim is to ensure that the butter is evenly distributed throughout so that the pastry rises and puffs up evenly when baked. Refrigerate until required.

Making puff pastry

Cut the dough with a pastry scraper, using a downward cutting motion.

Place the butter in the centre and fold over the arms to make a parcel.

Fold the top third of the pastry down and the bottom third up.

QUICK FLAKY PASTRY

Flaky pastry is a member of the puff pastry family. This is a very easy, quick version which will give you a crust with a nice flaky texture with some rise. It is important to use frozen butter and to handle the dough as little as possible. The butter is not worked into the dough at all but left in chunky grated pieces. If the butter starts to soften it is absorbed into the flour and the flakiness is lost. This is why it is important to keep the pastry chilled. The amount of pastry given here will make enough to cover two pies. Any leftover pastry can be used for decoration, or refrigerated for up to two days, or wrapped in plastic wrap and frozen for up to three months. This recipe makes about 600 g pastry.

1 Sift 350 g plain flour and ¹/₂ teaspoon salt into a large bowl. Grate 220 g frozen unsalted butter into the bowl using the large holes on a grater. Mix the butter gently into the flour with a knife, making sure all the pieces are coated in flour. Add 3 tablespoons chilled water and mix together with a metal spatula.
2 The pastry should come together in clumps. Test the dough by pinching a little piece of the dough between your fingers. If it doesn't hold together, mix in a teaspoon of iced water.
3 When the dough holds together, form it into a neat ball. Cover and refrigerate for 30 minutes, then roll out as required for your pie recipe.

USING READY-MADE PASTRY

For busy cooks, there is a large range of ready-made frozen or refrigerated pastries available at supermarkets. Standard puff and shortcrust pastries are available in blocks, and puff, butter puff and shortcrust pastries come as ready-rolled sheets. Allow frozen block pastry to thaw for two hours before using. Ready-rolled sheets take 5–10 minutes to thaw at room temperature.

ROLLING OUT DOUGH

To ensure good results.when rolling out pastry, there are a few things to keep in mind. Roll out the dough between two sheets of baking paper, or on a lightly floured surface. Always roll from the centre outwards, rotating the dough, rather than rolling backwards and forwards. Reduce the pressure towards the edges of the dough. If you used baking paper, remove the top sheet and carefully invert the pastry over the tin, then peel away the other sheet. Make sure you centre the pastry as it can't be moved once in place. Once the pastry is in the tin, quickly lift up the sides so they don't break over the edges of the tin. Use a small ball of excess dough to help ease and press the pastry shell into the sides of the tin. Cut away the excess pastry with a small, sharp knife. However gently you handle the dough it is bound to shrink slightly, so let it sit a little above the side of the tin. Refrigerate the pastry in the tin for 20 minutes to relax it and prevent or minimise shrinkage.

BLIND BAKING

If the pastry is to have a liquid filling, it usually requires blind baking, which means to partially cook the pastry without the filling to prevent the base becoming soggy. When blind baking, the pastry needs some weights put on it to prevent it rising. Cover the base and side of the pastry shell with crumpled baking or greaseproof paper. Pour in some baking beads, dried beans or uncooked rice. Bake for the recommended time (usually about 10 minutes) then remove the paper and beads and return the pastry to the oven for 10–15 minutes, or as specified in the recipe, until the base is dry with no greasy patches. Cool completely. The filling should also be cooled before placing it in the pastry shell.

WHEN READY TO BAKE

It is important to make sure you preheat the oven to the specified temperature before baking pastry.

Making quick flaky pastry

Using the large holes on the grater, grate the butter into the flour.

Mix the butter into the flour with a knife, making sure the butter is coated.

When the pastry comes together in clumps, form it into a ball.

SAVOURY PIES

OSSO BUCO AND GREMOLATA PIE

Preparation time: 40 minutes
Cooking time: 2 hours 50 minutes
Serves 4–6

1 kg veal shanks, each 3.5 cm thick
 (6 pieces)
plain flour, to coat
2 tablespoons olive oil
1 onion, finely chopped
1 carrot, finely chopped
1 celery stick, finely diced
2 cloves garlic, finely chopped
2/3 cup (170 ml) beef stock
400 g can chopped tomatoes
2/3 cup (170 ml) dry white wine
1 teaspoon dried oregano

Gremolata
4 tablespoons finely chopped
 fresh flat-leaf parsley
1–2 cloves garlic, finely chopped
1 tablespoon grated lemon rind

Parmesan polenta
1 cup (150 g) instant polenta
1/2 cup (125 ml) cream
1/2 cup (50 g) grated Parmesan

1 Coat the veal with flour. Heat
1 tablespoon of the oil in a large frying
pan over high heat. Cook and turn
the veal until brown, then set aside.
Preheat the oven to moderate 180°C
(350°F/Gas 4).

2 Heat the remaining oil in a 2 litre
flameproof casserole dish. Cook the
onion, carrot, celery and garlic over
low heat for 8 minutes, or until soft
but not brown.

3 Place the meat in a single layer on
top of the vegetables. Add the stock,
tomato, wine and oregano, and season
with salt and black pepper. Cover and
bake for 1 1/2–2 hours, or until the
meat is tender and falling off the bones
and the liquid reduced and thickened.

4 Using tongs, remove the bones and
any fatty sinew from the veal. If you
like the marrow, spoon it out and
return it to the pan. Spoon the hot
mixture evenly into an oval 1.25 litre
ovenproof dish. Combine the
gremolata ingredients and sprinkle
half over the filling.

5 Cook the polenta according to
manufacturer's instructions, then stir
in the cream and Parmesan. Season
with black pepper. Spread evenly
over the osso buco and rough up
with a fork. Bake for 25–30 minutes,
until bubbling. Leave for 5 minutes.
Sprinkle with the remaining gremolata.

NUTRITION PER SERVE (6)
Protein 42.5 g; Fat 17.5 g; Carbohydrate
23.5 g; Dietary Fibre 3.0 g; Cholesterol
171.5 mg; 1835 kJ (440 cal)

*When the meat is tender and falling off the
bones, remove the bones and fatty sinew.*

*Spread the polenta topping evenly over the
osso buco.*

CHICKEN, LEEK AND MUSHROOM PIES

Preparation time: 30 minutes
Cooking time: 1 hour
Makes 4

50 g butter
1 leek, thinly sliced
75 g Swiss brown mushrooms, sliced
1 tablespoon peanut oil
500 g chicken breast fillet, cut into
    2 cm pieces
1 tablespoon plain flour
1 cup (250 ml) chicken stock
150 g sliced ham, chopped
100 ml crème fraîche
1 tablespoon chopped fresh
    flat-leaf parsley
4 sheets ready-rolled frozen puff
    pastry, thawed
2 egg yolks, lightly beaten

1 Preheat the oven to moderate 180°C (350°F/Gas 4). Grease two baking trays and lightly dust with flour. Melt half of the butter in a frying pan and cook the leek over medium heat for 4–5 minutes, or until soft but not browned. Add the mushrooms and cook for 1 minute. Remove.
2 Heat the remaining butter and oil in the same pan and cook the chicken over medium–high heat in two batches until golden. Stir in the flour, cook for 1 minute, then stir in the stock. Return the leek and mushrooms to the pan and simmer over low heat, stirring often, for 10–15 minutes. Add the ham and the crème fraîche and cook for 5 minutes. Season. Stir in the parsley and cool completely.

3 Cut each pastry sheet into an 18 cm square, reserving the offcuts. Spoon filling into the centre of each square. Brush the edges with egg and bring them up over the filling, pinching them together. Cut out 16 large leaves from the offcuts and score veins on them. Carefully place a leaf over each seam. Brush with egg and bake for 20–25 minutes, or until golden.

NUTRITION PER PIE
Protein 39.5 g; Fat 74 g; Carbohydrate 64.5 g; Dietary Fibre 3.5 g; Cholesterol 301.5 mg; 4515 kJ (1080 cal)

Stir the chopped parsley into the creamy chicken mixture.

Bring the edges of the pastry squares up over the filling and pinch them together.

Place a pastry leaf over each seam on the top of each pie.

ASPARAGUS PIE

Preparation time: 40 minutes
+ 45 minutes refrigeration
Cooking time: 30 minutes
Serves 6

Pastry
350 g plain flour
250 g butter, chilled and cubed
2/3 cup (170 ml) iced water

800 g fresh asparagus
20 g butter
1/2 teaspoon chopped fresh thyme
1 French shallot, chopped
60 g sliced ham
1/3 cup (80 ml) cream
2 tablespoons grated Parmesan
1 egg
pinch of ground nutmeg
1 egg, extra, lightly beaten

1 To make the pastry, process the flour and a pinch of salt in a food processor for 3 seconds. Add the butter and mix until it is cut finely, but not entirely blended into the flour—a few lumps are desirable. With the motor running, gradually pour in the iced water until the dough comes together. It should still have some small pebbles of butter.

2 Transfer to a lightly floured work surface and press into a rectangle about 30 x 12 cm. Fold one end into the centre, then the opposite end over to cover the first. Roll into a rectangle again and repeat the folding three or four times. Wrap in plastic wrap and refrigerate for 45 minutes.

3 Trim the asparagus to 10 cm. Slice thick spears in half lengthways. Heat the butter in a large frying pan over medium heat and add the asparagus, thyme and shallot. Add a tablespoon of water and season with salt and pepper. Cook, stirring, for 3 minutes, or until the asparagus is tender.

4 Preheat the oven to moderately hot 200°C (400°F/Gas 6) and grease a 21 cm fluted, loose-based flan tin.

Roll the pastry out to a 2 mm thick circle with a diameter of about 30 cm. Line the flan tin and trim the pastry using kitchen scissors, leaving about 8 cm above the top of the tin. Place half the asparagus in one direction across the bottom of the dish. Layer the ham slices on top. Cover with the remaining asparagus, running in the opposite direction.

5 Combine the cream, Parmesan, egg and nutmeg and season. Pour over the asparagus. Fold the pastry over the filling, forming loose pleats. Brush with egg. Bake in the centre of the oven for 25 minutes, or until golden.

NUTRITION PER SERVE
Protein 15 g; Fat 46 g; Carbohydrate 45.5 g; Dietary Fibre 4 g; Cholesterol 200.5 mg; 2730 kJ (650 cal)

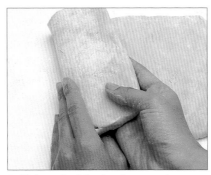

Fold the ends of the dough over and press into a rectangle.

Pour the combined cream, egg, Parmesan and nutmeg over the asparagus.

CHARGRILLED VEGETABLE AND PARMESAN PIE

Preparation time: 45 minutes
+ 1 hour standing
Cooking time: 1 hour 30 minutes
Serves 6

1 clove garlic, crushed
300 ml olive oil
2 large eggplants
1 large orange sweet potato
3 large zucchini
3 red capsicums
3 yellow capsicums
2 tablespoons polenta
3/4 cup (75 g) grated Parmesan
1 egg, lightly beaten

Pastry
450 g plain flour
2 teaspoons cumin seeds
2 teaspoons paprika
100 g butter, chopped

1 Place the garlic in a small bowl with the oil. Cut the eggplants and sweet potato into 5 mm slices and the zucchini into 5 mm lengths, then brush with the garlic oil. Quarter the capsicums, removing the seeds and membrane. Cook, skin-side-up, under a hot grill for 10 minutes, or until the skins blacken and blister. Cool in a plastic bag, then peel.

2 Chargrill the eggplant, orange sweet potato and zucchini in batches over high heat, turning occasionally, for 5–6 minutes, or until brown and tender. Set aside to cool.

3 Preheat the oven to moderate 180°C (350°F/Gas 4). Grease a deep 20 cm springform tin. Sift the flour into a bowl and add the cumin seeds, paprika and 1/2 teaspoon salt. Gently heat the butter in a saucepan with 225 ml water. Bring to the boil, pour into the flour and mix with a wooden spoon. When cool enough to handle, tip onto a floured surface and press gently together. Rest for 5 minutes.

4 Set aside one quarter of the dough and roll out the rest between two sheets of baking paper until large enough to cover the base and side of the tin. Line the tin, leaving some pastry overhanging. Sprinkle a layer of polenta over the base, then layer the red capsicum, zucchini, eggplant, sweet potato and yellow capsicum in the pie, brushing each layer with a little garlic oil, sprinkling with Parmesan and seasoning with salt and pepper as you go.

5 Roll out the remaining pastry between the baking paper to fit the top of the tin. Brush the edges of the bottom layer of pastry with egg. Cover with the pastry lid. Brush the edges with egg and trim with a sharp knife, crimping the edges to seal. Cut a small steam hole in the centre of the pie. Roll out the trimmings and use to decorate. Cook for 1 hour, or until crisp and golden (cover with foil if it browns too quickly). Cool for 1 hour. Serve at room temperature.

NUTRITION PER SERVE
Protein 18 g; Fat 54 g; Carbohydrate 67.5 g; Dietary Fibre 7 g; Cholesterol 86 mg; 3445 kJ (820 cal)

Layer the chargrilled vegetables and grated Parmesan in the pastry case.

LUXURY FISHERMAN'S PIE

Preparation time: 1 hour 10 minutes
Cooking time: 1 hour 10 minutes
Serves 6–8

1 kg raw medium prawns, peeled
   (heads and shells reserved)
1 1/2 cups (375 ml) fish stock
100 ml dry white wine
6 black peppercorns
1 bay leaf
1.5 kg potatoes (e.g. desiree or
   pontiac), cut into 3 cm pieces
100 ml milk
80 g butter
6 French shallots, chopped
1/3 cup (40 g) plain flour
300 ml cream
2 egg yolks
2 tablespoons chopped fresh flat-leaf
   parsley
500 g salmon fillet, skinned
   and boned
500 g firm white-fleshed fish fillets
   (e.g. ling, blue eye)
pinch of cayenne pepper

1 Place the prawn heads and shells in a saucepan with the fish stock, wine, peppercorns and bay leaf and bring to the boil over medium–high heat. Reduce the heat and simmer for 25 minutes, or until you have about 1 1/2 cups (375 ml). Strain into a bowl, discarding the solids.

2 Meanwhile, put the potatoes in a saucepan of cold water, bring to the boil, then reduce the heat and simmer for 10–12 minutes, or until cooked. Drain, then mash with a potato masher. Heat the milk and 50 g of the butter in a small saucepan over low heat, then slowly beat into the potato with a wooden spoon until smooth. Stir in 1/2 teaspoon salt.

3 Preheat the oven to moderate 180°C (350°F/Gas 4). Lightly grease a 4.25 litre ovenproof dish. Melt the remaining butter in a frying pan over medium heat, add the shallots and cook for 5 minutes, or until soft but not brown. Add the flour and cook for another minute. Gradually stir in the reserved prawn stock and cook for 2–3 minutes, or until thickened, then add half the cream and cook

for 5 minutes. Stir in the egg yolks and parsley and season.

4 Cut the fish into 2 cm chunks and place in the base of the ovenproof dish, along with the prawns. Cover with the sauce, then spread the potato on top and rough up with a fork. Drizzle with the remaining cream, allowing it to soak through the topping. Sprinkle with cayenne pepper and bake for 30 minutes, or until golden.

NUTRITION PER SERVE (8)
Protein 58.5 g; Fat 33 g; Carbohydrate 32 g; Dietary Fibre 3.5 g; Cholesterol 378.5 mg; 2790 kJ (665 cal)

Cover the combined fish pieces and prawns with the creamy sauce.

BACON, TURKEY AND CIDER PIE

Preparation time: 45 minutes
  + 20 minutes refrigeration
Cooking time: 4 hours
Serves 6

Pastry
3¼ cups (405 g) plain flour
1 teaspoon baking powder
200 g lard, chilled and roughly
  chopped
3–4 tablespoons iced water

4 carrots
4 celery sticks (including leafy tops)
9 spring onions
3 onions
1.5 kg smoked bacon bones
2 teaspoons whole black peppercorns
1.5 litres apple cider
500 g turkey breast fillet, cut into
  2 cm cubes
½ cup (60 g) seasoned plain flour
60 g butter
1 egg, lightly beaten

1 Sift the flour and baking powder into a large bowl and add the lard and ½ teaspoon salt. Rub the lard into the flour with your fingertips until the mixture resembles fine breadcrumbs. Make a well in the centre, add almost all the water and mix with a flat-bladed knife, using a cutting action, until the mixture comes together in beads, adding more water, a teaspoon at a time, if necessary. Turn out onto a lightly floured surface and gather together into a smooth ball. Flatten slightly into a disc, wrap in plastic wrap and refrigerate for at least 20 minutes.
2 Roughly chop two of the carrots, three of the celery sticks (including the leafy tops), six of the spring onions and cut two of the onions into quarters and place them in a large saucepan with the bacon bones, peppercorns, cider and 2 litres cold water. Bring to the boil over high heat, then reduce the heat and simmer for 2 hours. Remove the bones with tongs, then strain the

liquid into a bowl. Return the liquid to the saucepan and simmer for another hour, or until reduced (you will need 2 cups/500 ml). Meanwhile, pick the meat from the bacon bones, avoiding any gristle and small bones. You should have at least 200–250 g meat.
3 Cut the remaining carrots and celery sticks into 1 cm cubes, roughly chop the onion and cut the remaining spring onions into 3 cm lengths. Melt half the butter in a large frying pan over medium heat. Add the carrot and onion and cook for 5 minutes, or until the onion is soft and golden. Stir in the celery and spring onion and cook for another 3 minutes, or until all the vegetables have softened. Transfer to a plate.
4 Toss the turkey cubes in seasoned flour. Melt the remaining butter in the large frying pan over medium heat. Add the turkey and cook, turning constantly, for 8 minutes, or until browned all over. Return the vegetables and bacon meat to the pan and stir well, scraping the bottom of the pan to remove any flour. Slowly pour in the reserved stock. Stir for several minutes until the mixture has thickened, then remove from the heat and allow to cool.
5 Preheat the oven to moderate 180°C (350°F/Gas 4) and lightly grease a 25 cm ceramic pie dish. Divide the dough into two portions, one slightly larger than the other. Roll out the larger portion between two sheets of baking paper into a 35 cm circle, not too thin. Line the pie dish with the pastry. Spoon the filling into the shell. Roll out the remaining pastry between the baking paper to a 30 cm circle. Brush around the rim of the pastry base with egg, then place the top on. Trim off any excess pastry and pinch the edges together. If you wish, decorate the edges with pastry leaves. Brush the pie with egg, prick with a fork and bake for 45 minutes, or until golden.

NUTRITION PER SERVE
Protein 29 g; Fat 46 g; Carbohydrate 89.5 g; Dietary Fibre 6 g; Cholesterol 124 mg; 3715 kJ (885 cal)

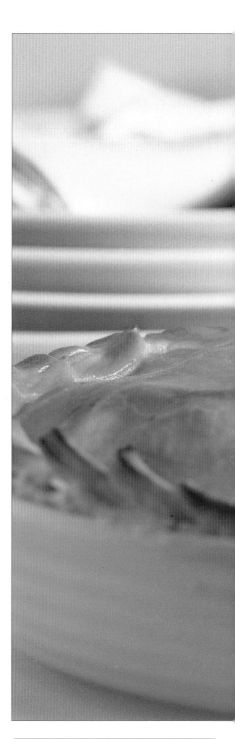

Gently gather the dough together into a smooth ball.

Using your fingers, remove the meat from the bacon bones.

Pour the reserved stock over the bacon and turkey mixture.

Brush the beaten egg over the rim of the filled pastry.

MINI SPINACH PIES

Preparation time: 45 minutes
  + 30 minutes cooling
Cooking time: 35 minutes
Makes 24

1/3 cup (80 ml) olive oil
2 onions, finely chopped
2 cloves garlic, chopped
150 g small button mushrooms,
  roughly chopped
200 g English spinach, chopped
1/2 teaspoon chopped fresh thyme
100 g feta, crumbled
750 g home-made or bought
  shortcrust pastry (see page 6)
milk, to glaze

1 Heat 2 tablespoons of the oil in a frying pan over medium heat, add the onion and garlic and cook for 5 minutes, or until soft and lightly coloured. Add the mushrooms and cook for another 4 minutes, or until softened. Transfer to a bowl.

2 Heat 1 tablespoon of the oil in the same pan over medium heat, add half the spinach and cook, stirring well, for 2–3 minutes, or until the spinach has softened. Add to the bowl with the onion. Repeat with the remaining oil and spinach. Add the thyme and feta to the bowl and mix. Season with salt and pepper and set aside to cool.

3 Preheat the oven to moderately hot 200°C (400°F/Gas 6) and grease two 12-hole round-based patty tins. Roll out half the pastry between two sheets of baking paper and cut out 24 rounds using a 7.5 cm cutter. Use these to line the patty tins, then divide the spinach mixture among the holes. Roll out the remaining pastry between the baking paper and cut into 24 x 7 cm rounds to fit the tops of the pies. Cover the pies with the lids and press the edges with a fork to seal. Prick the tops once with a fork, brush with milk and bake for 15–20 minutes, or until golden. Serve immediately or cool on a wire rack.

NUTRITION PER PIE
Protein 3 g; Fat 12 g; Carbohydrate 13.5 g; Dietary Fibre 1 g; Cholesterol 11.5 mg; 725 kJ (175 cal)

Cook the spinach in the oil until the spinach has softened.

Spoon the spinach mixture into the pastry-lined patty tins.

Seal the edges of the pies with a fork, then prick the tops once.

BRAISED LAMB SHANK PIE

Preparation time: 30 minutes
  + 2 hours refrigeration
Cooking time: 3 hours 10 minutes
Serves 6

8 lamb shanks
½ cup (60 g) seasoned plain flour
2 tablespoons olive oil
4 red onions, quartered
8 cloves garlic, peeled
1 cup (250 ml) full-bodied red wine
1 litre beef stock
2 tablespoons finely chopped fresh
  rosemary
6 whole black peppercorns
¼ cup (30 g) cornflour
375 g home-made or bought puff
  pastry (see page 8)
1 egg, lightly beaten

1 Preheat the oven to hot 220°C (425°F/Gas 7). Lightly dust the shanks in the seasoned flour, shaking off the excess. Heat the oil over medium heat in a large frying pan and cook the shanks for 2 minutes each side, or until well browned.

Transfer to a deep roasting tin and add the onion, garlic, wine, stock, rosemary and peppercorns. Cover with foil and bake for 1 hour.
2 Remove the foil, stir the mixture and return to the oven for 1 hour 10 minutes, stirring occasionally, until the meat falls off the bones.
3 Remove the lamb bones from the tin with tongs. Combine the cornflour with 2 tablespoons water, then stir into the tin. Return to the oven for 10 minutes, or until thickened. Transfer to a large bowl, allow to cool, then refrigerate for at least 2 hours, or overnight.
4 Preheat the oven to moderate 180°C (350°F/Gas 4). Grease a warm

23 cm pie plate with a rim, then fill with the meat mixture. Roll the pastry out between two sheets of baking paper until 3 cm wider than the plate. Cut a 2 cm strip around the edge of the pastry, brush with water and place damp-side-down on the rim. Cover with the pastry circle, pressing down on the edges. Use the back of a knife to make small slashes around the edge. Trim, then re-roll the scraps to decorate. Brush with egg and bake for 45 minutes, or until the pastry is golden and has risen.

NUTRITION PER SERVE
Protein 50.5 g; Fat 23.5 g; Carbohydrate 46.5 g; Dietary Fibre 3 g; Cholesterol 157.5 mg; 2625 kJ (630 cal)

Cook the lamb shanks until the meat falls off the bones.

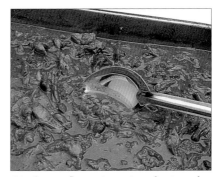

Stir the cornflour mixture into the tin and continue cooking until the sauce thickens.

SHEPHERD'S PIE

Preparation time: 30 minutes + cooling
Cooking time: 1 hour 35 minutes
Serves 6

¼ cup (60 ml) olive oil
1 large onion, finely chopped
2 cloves garlic, crushed
2 celery sticks, finely chopped
3 carrots, diced
2 bay leaves
1 tablespoon fresh thyme, chopped
1 kg good-quality lamb mince
1½ tablespoons plain flour
½ cup (125 ml) dry red wine
2 tablespoons tomato paste
400 g can crushed tomatoes
1.5 kg floury potatoes (e.g. desiree),
   cut into even-sized pieces
¼ cup (60 ml) milk
100 g butter
½ teaspoon ground nutmeg

1 Heat 2 tablespoons oil over medium heat in a large, heavy-based saucepan and cook the onion for 3–4 minutes, or until softened. Add the garlic, celery, carrot, bay leaves and thyme and cook for 2–3 minutes. Transfer to a bowl and remove the bay leaves.
2 Add the remaining oil to the same pan, add the mince and cook over high heat for 5–6 minutes, or until it changes colour. Mix in the flour, cook for 1 minute, then pour in the red wine and cook for 2–3 minutes. Return the vegetables to the pan with the tomato paste and crushed tomato. Reduce the heat, cover and simmer for 45 minutes, stirring occasionally. Season, to taste, then transfer to a shallow 3 litre ovenproof dish and leave to cool. Preheat the oven to moderate 180°C (350°F/Gas 4).
3 Meanwhile, boil the potatoes in salted water over medium heat for 20–25 minutes, or until tender. Drain, then mash with the milk and butter until smooth. Season with nutmeg and black pepper. Spoon over the mince and fluff with a fork. Bake for 30 minutes, or until golden and crusty.

NUTRITION PER SERVE
Protein 41.5 g; Fat 35 g; Carbohydrate 37 g; Dietary Fibre 6.5 g; Cholesterol 159 mg; 2700 kJ (645 cal)

Return the softened vegetables to the pan with the mince mixture.

Spoon the mashed potato over the cooked mince in the ovenproof dish.

CHICKEN AND CORN PIES

Preparation time: 25 minutes
  + 2 hours refrigeration
Cooking time: 50 minutes
Makes 6

1 tablespoon olive oil
650 g chicken thigh fillets, trimmed
    and cut into 1 cm pieces
1 tablespoon grated fresh ginger
400 g oyster mushrooms, halved
3 corn cobs, kernels removed
½ cup (125 ml) chicken stock
2 tablespoons kecap manis
2 tablespoons cornflour
90 g fresh coriander leaves, chopped
6 sheets ready-rolled shortcrust
    pastry
milk, to glaze

1 Grease six 12.5 cm (top) 9.5 cm (base) 3 cm (deep) metal pie tins. Heat the oil in a large frying pan over high heat and add the chicken. Cook for 5 minutes, or until golden. Add the ginger, mushrooms and corn and cook for 5–6 minutes, or until the chicken is just cooked through. Add the stock and kecap manis. Mix the cornflour with 2 tablespoons water in a small bowl or jug, then stir into the pan. Boil for 2 minutes before adding the coriander. Transfer to a bowl, cool a little then refrigerate for 2 hours, or until cold.

2 Preheat the oven to moderate 180°C (350°F/Gas 4). Using a saucer to guide you, cut a 15 cm round from each sheet of shortcrust pastry and line the six pie tins. Fill the shells with the cooled filling, then cut out another six rounds large enough to make the lids. Top the pies with the lids, cut away any extra pastry and seal the edges with a fork. Decorate the pies with shapes cut from pastry scraps. Prick a few holes in the top of each pie, brush with a little milk and bake for 35 minutes, or until golden.

NUTRITION PER PIE
Protein 35.5 g; Fat 57.5 g; Carbohydrate 84.5 g; Dietary Fibre 8 g; Cholesterol 144.5 mg; 4145 kJ (990 cal)

Boil the chicken and corn mixture for 2 minutes.

Cut out six rounds of pastry to fit the tops of the tins, then cover the filling.

TOURTIERE

Preparation time: 40 minutes
  + 20 minutes refrigeration
  + cooling
Cooking time: 1 hour
Serves 6

Pastry
2 1/4 cups (280 g) plain flour
1/2 teaspoon baking powder
120 g butter, chilled and cubed
1/2 teaspoon finely chopped
    fresh thyme
1 teaspoon lemon juice
1 egg, lightly beaten
1–2 tablespoons iced water

1 small carrot
1 baby fennel bulb, thick outer
    leaves removed
4 French shallots
20 g butter
200 g bacon, chopped
3 cloves garlic, crushed
500 g pork mince
1 teaspoon finely chopped fresh
    thyme
1 teaspoon finely chopped fresh sage
1/4 teaspoon ground nutmeg
3/4 cup (185 ml) chicken stock
250 g potatoes, cut into 2 cm cubes
1 egg, lightly beaten

1 To make the pastry, sift the flour, baking powder and 1/4 teaspoon salt into a large bowl and rub in the chilled butter with your fingertips until the mixture resembles fine breadcrumbs. Stir in the thyme, then make a well in the centre and add the lemon juice, egg and a little of the water. Mix with a flat-bladed knife, using a cutting action, until the mixture comes together in beads, adding more water if necessary.
2 Gently gather the dough together and lift out onto a lightly floured work surface. Press together into a ball and flatten slightly into a disc, wrap in plastic wrap and refrigerate for at least 20 minutes.
3 Finely chop the carrot, fennel and shallots in a food processor. Heat the butter in a large frying pan over

medium heat and add the chopped vegetables, bacon, garlic and mince. Cook, stirring often, for 10 minutes, or until the pork changes colour, then stir in the thyme, sage and nutmeg. Season well with salt and cracked black pepper. Add 1/4 cup (60 ml) of the stock and simmer for 10 minutes, or until it is absorbed. Set aside to cool.
4 Preheat the oven to moderately hot 200°C (400°F/Gas 6) and heat a baking tray. Grease a 23 cm (top) 18 cm (base) 3 cm (deep) pie dish. Place the remaining stock in a small saucepan with the potato and simmer for about 10 minutes, or until tender. Do not drain. Mash coarsely, then stir into the pork mixture.
5 Divide the dough into two portions, one slightly larger than the other. Roll out the larger portion between two sheets of baking paper until large enough to fit the base and side of the prepared dish. Line the dish. Spoon in the filling, levelling the surface. Brush the exposed pastry with beaten egg.
6 Roll out the remaining dough between the sheets of baking paper until large enough to cover the dish. Carefully cover the filling, trim the edges and crimp to seal. Brush the surface with egg and make 6–8 small slits over the surface. Bake on the hot baking tray on the centre shelf of the oven for about 30 minutes, or until golden.

NUTRITION PER SERVE
Protein 33 g; Fat 29.5 g; Carbohydrate 42 g; Dietary Fibre 3.5 g; Cholesterol 188.5 mg; 2350 kJ (560 cal)

COOK'S FILE
Note: The flavour of a tourtière improves over 24 hours and it is excellent served cold.

Use your fingers to remove the thick outer leaves from the baby fennel.

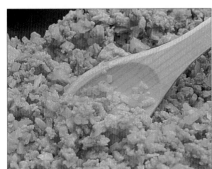

Cook the pork mixture, stirring often, until the pork changes colour.

Mash the potato and stock together, then stir into the pork mixture.

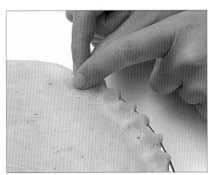

Trim the edges of the pastry and crimp them to seal.

BURGUNDY BEEF PIE

Preparation time: 30 minutes + cooling
Cooking time: 3 hours 10 minutes
Serves 6

2 tablespoons olive oil
40 g butter
185 g bacon, diced
1.25 kg chuck steak, trimmed and
    cut into 2.5 cm cubes
2 onions, diced
3 cloves garlic, crushed
2 carrots, cut into 1.5 cm cubes
¼ cup (30 g) plain flour
1¼ cups (315 ml) Burgundy
1½ cups (375 ml) beef stock
2 tablespoons tomato paste
1 teaspoon chopped fresh thyme
1 bay leaf
275 g small Swiss brown mushrooms,
    halved
pinch of ground nutmeg
3 tablespoons chopped fresh flat-leaf
    parsley
375 g home-made or bought puff
    pastry (see page 8)
1 egg, lightly beaten

1 Heat 1 tablespoon of oil and 20 g of butter in a large, heavy-based, flameproof casserole dish or saucepan over medium heat. Add the bacon and cook for 2–3 minutes. Transfer to a plate. Increase the heat to high, add the beef to the pan in batches and cook, turning, for 7–8 minutes, or until browned. Add to the bacon.
2 Heat the remaining oil in the pan over medium heat, add the onion and garlic and cook for 4–5 minutes. Add the carrot and cook, stirring once or twice, for 5 minutes. Stir in the flour, add the beef, bacon, wine, stock and tomato paste and stir for 5 minutes, or until the sauce has thickened slightly and is smooth. Add the thyme and bay leaf and season. Reduce the heat, cover and cook for 1¼ hours, or until the meat is tender, adding ¼ cup (60 ml) hot water, if necessary, to make a thick gravy.
3 Meanwhile, melt the remaining butter in a frying pan over low heat. Add the mushrooms and fry until

golden. Stir in the nutmeg and chopped parsley.
4 Preheat the oven to moderately hot 200°C (400°F/Gas 6) and grease a 2 litre oval ovenproof dish that has 5–6 cm sides. Roll out the pastry between two sheets of baking paper until about 6 mm thick and slightly larger than the dish. Roll out the scraps to a 35 x 10 cm strap, 4 mm thick. Cut into 1.5 cm wide strips.
5 Remove the bay leaf from the meat, then stir in the mushrooms. Spoon into the dish. Cover the dish

with the pastry lid, press the edges firmly down onto the lip of the dish, then trim off any excess. Brush the edges with egg. Make three 2.5 cm slits in the centre. Take a strip of pastry and twist a tight scroll. Repeat with the other strips. Run them around the rim, pressing joins together. Brush with egg and bake for 55–60 minutes, or until golden.

NUTRITION PER SERVE
Protein 58 g; Fat 34.5 g; Carbohydrate 31 g; Dietary Fibre 4 g; Cholesterol 220 mg; 2930 kJ (700 cal)

Cook the beef mixture until the sauce has thickened slightly and is smooth.

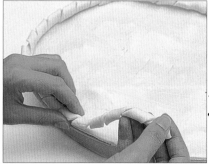
Twist the strips of pastry to form long, tight scrolls and place them around the pie rim.

SWEET POTATO AND FENNEL PIE

Preparation time: 20 minutes
    + 30 minutes refrigeration
    + 10 minutes draining
Cooking time: 1 hour 10 minutes
Serves 6

2 fennel bulbs (540 g), thick outer
    leaves removed, sliced
300 g sweet potato, cut into
    1 cm cubes
1 tablespoon dried juniper berries,
    ground
¼ cup (60 ml) olive oil
300 g ricotta
1 cup (100 g) grated Parmesan
100 g ground almonds
6 sheets ready-rolled shortcrust pastry
milk, to glaze
3 sheets ready-rolled puff pastry

1 Preheat the oven to moderate 180°C (350°F/Gas 4). Grease six 11 cm (top) 9.5 cm (base) and 2.5 cm (deep) pie tins. Place the fennel, sweet potato and ground juniper berries in a deep roasting tin and toss with the oil. Season, cover with foil and cook for 35 minutes, or until the vegetables have softened. Drain any oil away, transfer the vegetables to a bowl and refrigerate for 30 minutes, or until cold.
2 Combine the ricotta, Parmesan and ground almonds in a large bowl.

Transfer to a sieve and sit over a bowl for 10 minutes to drain away any liquid from the ricotta.
3 Cut a 15 cm round from each sheet of shortcrust pastry and line the pie tins, leaving the excess overhanging. Brush the rims with milk.
4 Divide the vegetables among the pastry shells, then top with ricotta mixture. Cut six 12 cm rounds from the puff pastry, place over the filled shells and trim. Seal the edges with a fork and prick a few holes in the tops. Brush with milk, then bake for 35 minutes, or until golden.

NUTRITION PER SERVE
Protein 29.5 g; Fat 86.5 g; Carbohydrate 104.5 g; Dietary Fibre 8.5 g; Cholesterol 102 mg; 5474 kJ (1310 cal)

Roast the fennel and sweet potato until they have softened.

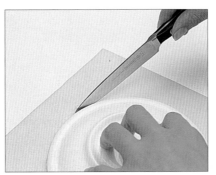

Cut a 15 cm round from each sheet of shortcrust, using a saucer to help you.

Spoon the ricotta and Parmesan mixture into the vegetable-filled pie tins.

MINI SEAFOOD AND FENNEL PIES

Preparation time: 20 minutes
  + cooling time
Cooking time: 40 minutes
Makes 6

50 g butter
1 fennel bulb, chopped, 1 teaspoon
  leaves reserved and chopped
1 clove garlic, crushed
3 tablespoons finely chopped French
  shallots
1½ tablespoons plain flour
½ cup (125 ml) cream
1 teaspoon Pernod (optional)
pinch of cayenne pepper
350 g small raw prawns, peeled
170 g fresh scallops
600 g home-made or bought
  shortcrust pastry (see page 6)
1 egg, lightly beaten

1 Melt the butter in a large frying pan over medium heat. Add the fennel, garlic and shallots and gently cook, stirring, for 6–8 minutes, or until softened but not browned. Stir in the flour, cook for 20–30 seconds, then gradually add the cream and Pernod. Cook, stirring, until very thick. Add the cayenne pepper and season with salt and pepper. Stir the prawns, scallops and reserved fennel leaves into the mixture, then remove from the heat and set aside to cool.
2 Preheat the oven to moderate 180°C (350°F/Gas 4) and heat a baking tray. Grease six 11 cm (top) 6 cm (base) 2 cm (deep) pie tins. Divide the pastry into six and roll two-thirds of each portion out to a size large enough to fit the base and side of the tins. Line the tins with the pastry. Roll the remaining portions to a size large enough to form pie lids.
3 Divide the filling among the tins. Brush the pastry rims with egg. Top each with a lid, pressing the edges firmly. Trim with a sharp knife and seal with a fork. Brush with egg. Make a cross-hatch pattern over the tops using the fork—two lines in each direction—then make an incision in the middle. Place on the hot tray and bake for 25 minutes, or until the pastry is golden.

NUTRITION PER PIE
Protein 23.5 g; Fat 42.5 g; Carbohydrate 45.5 g; Dietary Fibre 3 g; Cholesterol 204 mg; 2735 kJ (655 cal)

COOK'S FILE
Note: If small prawns aren't available, cut larger ones into 2.5 cm lengths. If you would prefer to discard the scallop coral, buy extra scallops to make up the weight.

Spoon the cooled seafood filling into the pastry-lined tins.

Make a cross-hatch pattern on the pastry, then make an incision in the middle.

BEEF, STOUT AND POTATO PIE

Preparation time: 30 minutes
Cooking time: 3 hours 10 minutes
Serves 6

2 tablespoons olive oil
1.25 kg chuck steak, cut into
    3 cm cubes, excess fat trimmed
2 onions, sliced
2 rashers bacon, roughly chopped
4 cloves garlic, crushed
2 tablespoons plain flour
440 ml can stout
1½ cups (375 ml) beef stock
1½ tablespoons chopped fresh thyme
2 large potatoes, thinly sliced
olive oil, for brushing

1 Heat 1 tablespoon of the oil over high heat in a large, heavy-based flameproof casserole dish, add the beef in batches and cook, turning occasionally, for 5 minutes, or until the meat is nicely coloured. Remove from the dish. Reduce the heat to low, add the remaining oil to the dish, then cook the onion and bacon for 10 minutes, stirring occasionally. Add the garlic and cook for another minute. Return the beef to the pan.
2 Sprinkle the flour over the beef, cook for a minute, stirring, and then gradually add the stout, stirring constantly. Add the stock, increase the heat to medium–high and bring to the boil. Stir in the thyme, season well, then reduce the heat and simmer for 2 hours, or until the beef is tender and the mixture has thickened.
3 Preheat the oven to moderately hot 200°C (400°F/Gas 6). Lightly grease a 1.25 litre ovenproof dish and pour in the beef mixture. Arrange potato slices in a single overlapping layer over the top to cover the meat. Brush with olive oil and sprinkle with salt. Bake for 30–40 minutes, or until the potato is golden.

NUTRITION PER SERVE
Protein 48.5 g; Fat 13 g; Carbohydrate 14 g; Dietary Fibre 2 g; Cholesterol 146 mg; 1665 kJ (400 cal)

Gradually add the stout to the beef mixture, stirring constantly.

Arrange the potato slices in a single overlapping layer to cover the meat.

More than a basic meat pie

For pie lovers, nothing surpasses a plain meat pie. Quick variations of the basic pie can be made by adding a few extra ingredients such as chopped mushrooms or bacon, as well as spices. Toppings can also be varied—mashed potato, for instance, is a popular choice.

MEAT PIE

Preparation time: 25 minutes + cooling
Total cooking time: 55 minutes
Makes 4

1 tablespoon olive oil
1 onion, finely chopped
1 clove garlic, crushed
500 g beef mince
2 tablespoons plain flour

¾ cup (185 ml) beef stock
2 tablespoons tomato paste
1 tablespoon Worcestershire sauce
4 sheets frozen shortcrust pastry, thawed
beaten egg, to glaze

1 Heat the oil in a frying pan, add the onion and cook for 5 minutes, or until softened. Add the garlic and cook for another minute. Add the beef mince and cook over medium heat for 5–7 minutes, or until the mince is browned, breaking up any lumps with a fork.

2 Sprinkle the flour over the meat and stir to combine. Cook for 1 minute, then add the stock, tomato paste, Worcestershire sauce, ¼ teaspoon salt and some pepper and stir for 2 minutes. Bring to the boil, then reduce the heat slightly and simmer for 10 minutes, or until the mixture has thickened. Cool completely.

3 Preheat the oven to hot 210°C (415°F/Gas 6–7). Place a large baking tray into the oven to heat. Grease four 11 cm pie tins. Cut out four 14 cm rounds from the pastry, line the pie tins, then cut four 11.5 cm rounds as lids. Spoon the filling into the pastry cases, put the lids on and seal with beaten egg. Pinch the pastry cases and lids together. Decorate with pastry scraps, brush with the egg and pierce the tops with a fork. Bake on the hot baking tray for 30 minutes, or until the pastry is crisp and brown.

CURRY PIE

Add 1 teaspoon Madras curry powder and, from a can, 2 whole, peeled tomatoes, crushed, to the basic meat mixture and proceed with the recipe.

POTATO PIE

Make the basic meat recipe. Line the pastry cases with pastry. You will only need 2 sheets of frozen pastry. Roughly chop 5 large potatoes and cook in a saucepan of boiling water for 10–15 minutes, or until soft, then drain thoroughly and mash with a potato masher. Add ¼ cup (60 ml) milk and 45 g butter to the potato and beat in with a wooden spoon until smooth. Fill the pastry bases with the meat mixture and top the pies with the potato mixture—you can either spread it or, for an attractive effect, pipe it on. Bake for 20–25 minutes, or until the potato topping is lightly golden. This much-loved topping is a delicious variation on pastry.

BACON PIE

Cook 200 g chopped bacon with the onion as in the original recipe. Don't add any extra salt as the bacon will make the filling salty enough. Follow the recipe as described above.

MUSHROOM PIE

Roughly chop 150 g button mushrooms. Heat 2 tablespoons oil in a frying pan, add the mushrooms and cook for 5 minutes, or until they are golden. Add to the meat mixture before filling the pies, then proceed with the recipe.

Clockwise from back: Curry pie; Potato pie; Basic meat pie; Bacon pie; Mushroom pie

RABBIT AND MUSHROOM PIE WITH POLENTA LID

Preparation time: 30 minutes
  + 15 minutes soaking
Cooking time: 1 hour 20 minutes
Serves 4–6

10 g dried porcini mushrooms
80 g butter
1 kg trimmed rabbit meat, cut into
    2.5 cm cubes (buy fillets or
    de-boned saddles)
200 g piece pancetta or bacon, diced
1 large onion, finely chopped
200 g button mushrooms, quartered
150 g shimeji mushrooms, trimmed
1 tablespoon plain flour
200 ml crème fraîche
150 ml cream
2 teaspoons chopped fresh thyme
2 tablespoons chopped fresh flat-leaf
    parsley

Topping
2 cups (500 ml) milk
20 g butter
1/2 cup (75 g) instant polenta
1/2 cup (50 g) shredded Parmesan

pinch of ground nutmeg
1 egg, lightly beaten

1 Soak the porcini mushrooms in 1/2 cup (125 ml) warm water for 15 minutes. Heat half the butter in a large, deep frying pan over medium heat and cook the rabbit in batches for 5 minutes each batch, or until brown all over. Remove from the pan. Add the pancetta to the pan and cook for 4–5 minutes, or until golden. Add the remaining butter and the onion, reduce the heat and cook for 5 minutes, or until softened.
2 Add the button and shimeji mushrooms to the pan and stir well. Squeeze dry the porcini mushrooms and chop. Add to the pan, along with the liquid. Simmer for 10 minutes, or until all the liquid evaporates. Add the flour and stir for 1 minute. Stir in the crème fraîche and cream and season with pepper. Return the rabbit to the pan and simmer for 20 minutes, or until the sauce has reduced and thickened. Add the fresh herbs.
3 Preheat the oven to moderately hot 200°C (400°F/Gas 6). Grease a 1.25 litre ovenproof dish. Spoon

in the rabbit and mushroom filling.
4 To make the topping, put the milk, butter and 1/2 teaspoon salt in a saucepan and heat until almost boiling. Add the polenta and stir constantly for 5 minutes, or until thick and smooth and the mixture pulls away from the sides. Remove from the heat and stir in the Parmesan. Add the nutmeg, beat in the egg and season. Spread over the rabbit mixture and bake for 20 minutes, or until golden.

NUTRITION PER SERVE (6)
Protein 57 g; Fat 53 g; Carbohydrate 9.5 g; Dietary Fibre 2.5 g; Cholesterol 282 mg; 3260 kJ (780 cal)

Use a wooden spoon to spread the polenta topping over the rabbit mixture.

MINI THAI CHICKEN PIES

Preparation time: 15 minutes
  + 20 minutes refrigeration + cooling
Cooking time: 35 minutes
Makes 24

Pastry
4 cups (500 g) plain flour
250 g butter, chilled and cubed
1 teaspoon chilli flakes, toasted
4–6 tablespoons iced water

1 tablespoon peanut oil
4 spring onions, finely chopped
2 cloves garlic, crushed
1 stem lemon grass (white part only),
  finely chopped
1 tablespoon green curry paste
500 g chicken thigh fillets, trimmed
  and finely diced
1 tablespoon plain flour
1/3 cup (90 ml) coconut cream
2 tablespoons finely chopped
  fresh coriander
1 teaspoon grated palm sugar or
  soft brown sugar
2 teaspoons fish sauce
2 teaspoons lime juice
1 egg, lightly beaten

1 Sift the flour into a large bowl and rub in the butter with your fingertips until the mixture resembles fine breadcrumbs. Stir in the chilli flakes. Make a well in the centre, add almost all the water and mix with a flat-bladed knife, using a cutting action, until the mixture comes together in beads. Add more water if needed.
2 Gather the dough together and lift onto a lightly floured work surface. Press into a ball, cut in half, then flatten each portion into a disc and wrap in plastic wrap. Refrigerate for at least 20 minutes.
3 Preheat the oven to moderately hot 200°C (400°F/Gas 6). Place a baking tray in the oven to heat. Lightly grease two 12-hole shallow, round-based patty tins. Heat the oil in a large, deep frying pan over medium heat and cook the spring onion, garlic and lemon grass for 1 minute. Stir in the curry paste and

cook for 1 minute, or until fragrant.
4 Increase the heat to high. Add the chicken and cook for 4–5 minutes, or until cooked. Reduce the heat to medium, stir in the flour and cook for 1 minute. Pour in the coconut cream and simmer for 2–3 minutes, or until thick. Add the coriander, sugar, fish sauce and lime juice, then set aside to cool.
5 Roll one portion of the dough out between two sheets of baking paper until 2 mm thick. Remove the top sheet of paper and, using a 7.5 cm cutter, cut out 24 rounds. Gently place into the tins. Spoon the cooled filling into the rounds to come up to the top. Roll out the remaining pastry to 2 mm thick and, using a 7 cm cutter, cut out 24 rounds. Brush the edges with egg, place the pastry lids over the filling and press the edges

together with a fork. Lightly brush with beaten egg, prick with a fork, place on the hot tray and bake for 15–20 minutes, or until golden.

NUTRITION PER PIE
Protein 6.5 g; Fat 12 g; Carbohydrate 16.5 g; Dietary Fibre 1 g; Cholesterol 52.5 mg; 840 kJ (200 cal)

Carefully spoon the cooled filling into the pastry rounds.

MOROCCAN LAMB PIE

Preparation time: 30 minutes + cooling
Cooking time: 2 hours 40 minutes
Serves 6–8

¼ cup (60 ml) olive oil
2 onions, finely chopped
4 cloves garlic, crushed
1¼ teaspoons ground cinnamon
1¼ teaspoons ground cumin
1¼ teaspoons ground coriander
½ teaspoon ground ginger
large pinch of cayenne pepper
1.2 kg boned lamb leg, trimmed and
    cut into 2 cm cubes
1½ cups (375 ml) chicken stock
2 teaspoons grated lemon rind
1 tablespoon lemon juice
2 carrots, cut into 1.5 cm cubes
⅓ cup (35 g) ground almonds
½ cup (25 g) chopped fresh
    coriander
500 g home-made or bought puff
    pastry (see page 8)
1 egg, lightly beaten

1 Heat the oil in a large saucepan.
Add the onion, garlic, cinnamon,
cumin, ground coriander, ginger and
cayenne pepper and cook, stirring,
over medium heat for 30–40 seconds.
Add the lamb and stir until coated in
the spices. Add the stock, lemon rind
and lemon juice and cook, covered,
over low heat for 45 minutes.
2 Add the carrot, cover and simmer
for another 45 minutes, or until the
lamb is tender. Stir in the almonds,
increase the heat and boil, uncovered,
for 30 minutes, or until the sauce
becomes very thick. Stir in the fresh
coriander, season to taste, and cool.
3 Preheat the oven to moderately
hot 200°C (400°F/Gas 6) and heat
a baking tray. Grease a 25 cm (top)
20 cm (base) 4 cm (deep) pie dish.
Roll out the pastry to a 42 cm round
and neaten the edge with a sharp
knife. Line the dish with the pastry,
with the excess hanging over.
4 Spoon the filling into the dish,
levelling the surface. Fold the
overhanging pastry up and over,
forming pleats, to encase most of

the filling, leaving an opening in the
centre. Using kitchen scissors, cut
out Vs of pastry where it falls into
deep folds towards the middle. This
reduces the thickness so that the
pastry can bake evenly.
5 Brush with egg and bake on the
hot tray in the centre of the oven for

20 minutes. Reduce the oven to
moderate 180°C (350°F/Gas 4),
cover the pie with foil and bake
for another 20 minutes.

NUTRITION PER SERVE (8)
Protein 39 g; Fat 30.5 g; Carbohydrate
26 g; Dietary Fibre 3 g; Cholesterol
114.5 mg; 2230 kJ (535 cal)

*Boil the lamb mixture for 30 minutes, or
until the sauce becomes very thick.*

*Fold the overhanging pastry up and over to
encase most of the filling.*

SALMON FILO PIE WITH DILL BUTTER

Preparation time: 25 minutes + cooling
Cooking time: 50 minutes
Serves 6

¾ cup (150 g) medium-grain
    white rice
80 g butter, melted
8 sheets filo pastry
500 g fresh salmon fillet, skin
    and bones removed, cut into
    1.5 cm chunks
2 French shallots, finely chopped
1½ tablespoons baby capers
150 g Greek-style yoghurt
1 egg
1 tablespoon grated lemon rind
3 tablespoons chopped fresh dill
¼ cup (25 g) dry breadcrumbs
1 tablespoon sesame seeds
2 teaspoons lemon juice

1 Put the rice in a large saucepan
and add enough water to cover the
rice by 2 cm. Bring to the boil over
medium heat, then reduce the heat to
low, cover and cook for 20 minutes,
or until all the water has been
absorbed and tunnels appear on the
surface of the rice. Set aside to cool.
2 Preheat the oven to moderate
180°C (350°F/Gas 4). Grease a 20 x
30 cm tin with melted butter. Cover
the sheets of pastry with a damp tea
towel. Put the salmon in a large
bowl with the shallots, capers, rice,
yoghurt and egg. Add the lemon rind,
1 tablespoon of the dill and season
with salt and pepper.
3 Layer four sheets of pastry in the
base of the tin, brushing each one
with melted butter and leaving the
sides of the pastry overlapping the
side of the tin. Spoon the salmon
mixture on top and pat down well.
Fold in the excess pastry.

Top with four more sheets of filo,
brushing each one with melted
butter and sprinkling all but the
top layer with a tablespoon of
breadcrumbs. Sprinkle the top
layer with sesame seeds.
4 Score the top of the pie into
diamonds without cutting right
through the pastry. Bake for
25–30 minutes on the lowest
shelf until golden brown. Reheat
the remaining butter, add the lemon
juice and remaining dill and pour
some over each portion of pie.

NUTRITION PER SERVE
Protein 23 g; Fat 19.5 g; Carbohydrate
34.5 g; Dietary Fibre 1 g; Cholesterol
109.5 mg; 1705 kJ (410 cal)

Combine the salmon, shallots, capers, rice, yoghurt, egg, lemon rind and dill.

Sprinkle the pie with sesame seeds, then score the top into diamonds.

RAISED GAME PIE

Preparation time: 50 minutes
+ overnight setting
+ cooling
Cooking time: 4 hours 40 minutes
Serves 4–6

Jelly
any bones reserved from the
    game meat
2 pig's trotters
1 onion, quartered
1 carrot, roughly chopped
1 celery stick, chopped
2 bay leaves
6 black peppercorns

Filling
250 g pork belly, diced into 5 mm
    pieces
4 rashers streaky bacon, chopped
400 g game meat (e.g. rabbit,
    pheasant), removed from carcass
    and finely cut into 5 mm dice
    (bones reserved)
½ small onion, finely chopped
½ teaspoon ground nutmeg
½ teaspoon ground cinnamon
2 dried juniper berries, crushed
1 teaspoon chopped fresh thyme

Pastry
4 cups (500 g) plain flour
80 g lard
1 egg, lightly beaten

1 To make the stock for the jelly, place all the ingredients and 1.75 litres water in a large saucepan and bring to the boil over high heat. Remove any scum that may have risen. Reduce the heat and simmer for 3 hours, skimming off any scum that forms on top. Strain and return to the pan and reduce until you have about 2 cups (500 ml) of stock. Allow to cool, thenrefrigerate.
2 To make the filling, combine all the ingredients in a bowl. Season.
3 To make the pastry, sift the flour and ½ teaspoon salt into a large bowl and make a well in the centre. Bring 200 ml water and the lard to the boil in a saucepan. Pour the boiling liquid into the flour and mix with a wooden spoon to form a dough. Gather together and lift onto a lightly floured work surface. Press together until smooth. Keep the dough warm by covering with foil and putting it in a warm place.
4 Preheat the oven to moderately hot 190°C (375°F/Gas 5). Grease an 18 cm springform tin. While the pastry is still warm, roll out two-thirds of the dough between two sheets of baking paper and line the base and side of the tin, leaving some overhanging. Spoon the filling into the tin, pressing down well. Roll out the remaining dough to about 4 mm thick and 20 cm across. Place on top of the tin and pinch the edges together to seal. Trim the edges and cut a small hole in the top of the pie.
5 Roll out any remaining dough, cut it into decorative shapes and stick them into place on the pie using beaten egg. Glaze the top with egg and bake for 1 hour 20 minutes— cover the top with foil after about 45 minutes to prevent it colouring too much.
6 Remove the pie from the oven and allow to cool for about 25 minutes. Gently remove from the tin, brush the top and sides with beaten egg and place on a baking tray. Return to the oven and cook for another 20 minutes until the surface is nicely coloured and is firm to touch. Remove from the oven and allow to cool.
7 Warm the jelly to a pouring consistency. Place a small piping nozzle into the hole in the pie and pour in a little of the jelly. Leave to settle, then pour in more jelly until the pie is full. Fill the pie completely so there are no gaps when the jelly sets. Refrigerate overnight. Return to room temperature for serving.

NUTRITION PER SERVE (6)
Protein 39.5 g; Fat 20 g; Carbohydrate 62.5 g; Dietary Fibre 3.5 g; Cholesterol 112.5 mg; 2455 kJ (585 cal)

COOK'S FILE
Note: If there is some jelly left, you can freeze it and use it to add flavour to soups, casseroles or sauces.

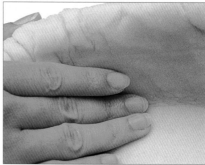

Line the tin with the warm pastry, leaving some overhanging.

Place the dough on top of the filling and pinch the edges together to seal.

Use a small, sharp knife to cut a small hole in the top of the pie.

Insert a nozzle into the hole and pour in a little of the liquid jelly.

35

CHILLI CON CARNE PIE

Preparation time: 25 minutes
  + 20 minutes refrigeration
Cooking time: 2 hours 15 minutes
Serves 6–8

Pastry
1½ cups (185 g) plain flour
100 g butter, chilled and cubed
¾ cup (90 g) grated Cheddar
1–2 tablespoons iced water

2 tablespoons olive oil
1 onion, chopped
2 cloves garlic, chopped
¼ teaspoon chilli powder
2 teaspoons ground cumin
1 teaspoon ground coriander
¼ teaspoon cayenne pepper
1 teaspoon paprika
1 teaspoon dried oregano
750 g beef mince
2 tablespoons tomato paste
½ cup (125 ml) dry red wine
425 g can crushed tomatoes
1 tablespoon wholegrain mustard
290 g can red kidney beans, drained
  and rinsed
2 tablespoons chopped fresh
  flat-leaf parsley
1 tablespoon chopped fresh oregano
⅔ cup (160 g) sour cream

1 Sift the flour into a bowl and rub in the butter with your fingertips until the mixture resembles fine breadcrumbs. Stir in the cheese. Make a well and add almost all the water. Mix with a flat-bladed knife, using a cutting action, until the dough comes together, adding more water if necessary.
2 Gather the dough together and lift out onto a lightly floured surface. Press it into a ball and flatten slightly into a disc. Cover in plastic wrap and refrigerate for at least 20 minutes.
3 Heat the oil in a large saucepan over medium heat and cook the onion for 5 minutes, or until softened. Add the garlic, spices and dried oregano and cook for 2 minutes. Add the mince and cook over high heat for 5 minutes, or until brown. Stir in the tomato paste and cook for

1 minute. Pour in the wine and simmer for 3 minutes. Add the tomato and mustard, bring to the boil, then reduce the heat and simmer for 30 minutes.
4 Add the kidney beans to the beef and cook for 30 minutes, or until any excess moisture has evaporated. Stir in the fresh herbs. Season, to taste.
5 Preheat the oven to moderately hot 200°C (400°F/Gas 6). Lightly grease a 23 cm (top) 18 cm (base) 3 cm (deep) pie dish, then fill with beef mixture. Roll out the pastry to fit

the top of the dish, then place over the top and trim and crimp the edges. Make two or three steam vents, bake for 10 minutes, then reduce the oven to moderate 180°C (350°F/Gas 4) and cook for 40–45 minutes, or until the top is golden. Cover the top with foil if it is browning too much. Serve with sour cream.

NUTRITION PER SERVE (8)
Protein 27 g; Fat 32 g; Carbohydrate 24 g; Dietary Fibre 4 g; Cholesterol 110.5 mg; 2085 kJ (500 cal)

Simmer the mixture until the excess liquid has evaporated.

Use a rolling pin to help you roll the pastry over the filling.

SPINACH PIE

Preparation time: 30 minutes
  + 30 minutes refrigeration
  + 10 minutes standing
Cooking time: 55 minutes
Serves 8–10

Pastry
2 cups (250 g) plain flour
1/3 cup (80 ml) olive oil
1 egg, beaten
4–5 tablespoons iced water

1 kg spinach (silverbeet), stalks
  removed, roughly chopped
1 tablespoon olive oil
1 large leek, sliced
4 cloves garlic, crushed
2 cups (500 g) ricotta
1 cup (90 g) grated pecorino cheese
300 g feta, crumbled
3 eggs, lightly beaten
3 tablespoons chopped fresh dill
1/2 cup (15 g) chopped fresh flat-leaf
  parsley

1 Sift the flour and 1/2 teaspoon salt
into a large bowl and make a well in
the centre. Mix the oil, egg and most
of the water, add to the flour and mix
with a flat-bladed knife until the
mixture comes together in beads,
adding a little more water if
necessary. Gather the dough and
press into a ball. Wrap in plastic
wrap and refrigerate for about
30 minutes. (Pastry made with
oil needs to be well chilled.)
2 Place the spinach in a large
saucepan, sprinkle lightly with water,
then cover and steam for 5 minutes,
stirring occasionally, until wilted.
Drain, squeeze out excess moisture,
then finely chop.
3 Preheat the oven to moderately
hot 200°C (400°F/Gas 6) and heat a
baking tray. Grease a round, fluted
tart tin with a removable base, 25 cm
(top) 23 cm (base) 4 cm (deep).
Heat the oil in a frying pan, add
the leek and garlic and cook over
low–medium heat for 5 minutes, or
until soft. Place in a large bowl with
the ricotta, pecorino, feta, spinach,
egg, dill and parsley. Season and mix.
4 Roll out two-thirds of the pastry
between two sheets of baking paper
until large enough to fit the tart tin.

Line the tin, then fill with spinach
mixture. Roll out the remaining
pastry between the baking paper and
place over the mixture. Trim the
edges and make two or three small
slits to allow the steam to escape.
5 Bake the pie on the hot tray for
15 minutes, then reduce the oven to
moderate 180°C (350°F/Gas 4) and
cook for another 30 minutes. Cover
the top of the pie with foil if it is
browning too much. Stand for
5–10 minutes before slicing.

NUTRITION PER SERVE (10)
Protein 20 g; Fat 26.5 g; Carbohydrate
20.5 g; Dietary Fibre 4 g; Cholesterol
123.5 mg; 1660 kJ (395 cal)

*Drain the wilted silverbeet well, then finely
chop with a large, sharp knife.*

COCKTAIL LEEK PIES

Preparation time: 20 minutes + cooling
Cooking time: 35 minutes
Makes 32

60 g butter
2 tablespoons olive oil
1 onion, finely chopped
3 leeks, finely sliced
1 clove garlic, chopped
1 tablespoon plain flour
2 tablespoons sour cream
1 cup (100 g) grated Parmesan
1 teaspoon chopped fresh thyme
4 sheets frozen puff pastry, thawed
1 egg, lightly beaten

1 Heat the butter and oil in a large frying pan over medium heat. Add the onion and cook, stirring occasionally, for 2 minutes. Add the leek and garlic and cook for 5 minutes, or until the leek is softened and lightly coloured. Add the flour and stir into the mixture for 1 minute. Add the sour cream and stir until slightly thickened. Transfer to a bowl and add the Parmesan and thyme. Season with salt and cracked black pepper and allow to cool.
2 Preheat the oven to moderately hot 200°C (400°F/Gas 6). Place a lightly greased baking tray in the oven to heat. Using a 6 cm cutter, cut the pastry into 64 circles. Place

2 heaped teaspoons of filling on half the pastry circles, leaving a small border. Lightly brush the edges with egg, then place a pastry circle on top of each. Seal the edges well with a fork. Lightly brush the tops with egg. Place the pies on the heated tray and bake for 25 minutes, or until the pies are puffed and golden.

NUTRITION PER PIE
Protein 2.5 g; Fat 9 g; Carbohydrate 8.5 g; Dietary Fibre 0.5 g; Cholesterol 19.5 mg; 510 kJ (120 cal)

Stir the sour cream through the leek mixture until slightly thickened.

Place 2 heaped teaspoons of filling on half of the pastry circles.

Place the remaining pastry circles on top of the filling and seal the edges well.

VEAL PIE WITH JERUSALEM ARTICHOKE AND POTATO TOPPING

Preparation time: 30 minutes
  + 10 minutes standing
Cooking time: 1 hour 15 minutes
Serves 4–6

1 tablespoon olive oil
500 g lean veal mince
2 onions, finely chopped
3 cloves garlic, crushed
150 g bacon, diced
½ teaspoon dried rosemary
2 tablespoons plain flour
pinch of cayenne pepper
½ cup (125 ml) dry white wine
150 ml cream
1 egg, lightly beaten
2 hard-boiled eggs,
   roughly chopped

Topping

500 g Jerusalem artichokes,
   peeled
400 g potatoes, cut into large cubes
100 g butter, chopped

1 To make the filling, heat the oil in a large frying pan over medium heat and add the mince, onion, garlic, bacon and rosemary. Cook, stirring often, for 10 minutes, or until the veal changes colour. Stir in the flour and cayenne pepper and cook for 1 minute. Pour in the wine and ½ cup (125 ml) water. Season well. Simmer for 5 minutes, or until the sauce is very thick, then stir in the cream, beaten egg and chopped egg.
2 Preheat the oven to hot 210°C (415°F/Gas 6–7). Lightly grease a 21 cm springform tin. To make the topping, boil the artichokes and

potato together for 12–15 minutes, or until tender. Drain, return to the pan, add the butter, then mash until smooth. Season, to taste.
3 Spoon the filling into the tin and level the surface. Spread the topping over the veal. Bake for 15 minutes, then reduce the heat to moderate 180°C (350°F/Gas 4) and bake for another 30 minutes, or until the topping is set and golden. Rest in the tin for 10 minutes before serving.

NUTRITION PER SERVE (6)
Protein 31.5 g; Fat 37.5 g; Carbohydrate 17 g; Dietary Fibre 4 g; Cholesterol 258 mg; 2265 kJ (540 cal)

When the sauce has thickened, stir in the cream, beaten egg and chopped egg.

Mash the potato and artichoke mixture until smooth.

LITTLE CHICKEN AND VEGETABLE POT PIES

Preparation time: 45 minutes
+ 20 minutes refrigeration
Cooking time: 1 hour 20 minutes
Makes 6

Pastry

1 1/4 cups (155 g) plain flour
90 g butter, chilled and cubed
1 tablespoon finely chopped
fresh thyme
1 tablespoon finely chopped
fresh flat-leaf parsley
3–4 tablespoons iced water

Filling

750 g chicken breast fillets
1 lemon, quartered
5 spring onions
2 bay leaves
1 1/2 cups (375 ml) chicken stock
1/4 cup (60 ml) dry white wine
50 g butter
1 large onion, thinly sliced
1 tablespoon finely chopped fresh
tarragon
100 g button mushrooms, thinly
sliced
3/4 cup (90 g) plain flour
2 large carrots, cut into 1 cm
cubes
1 celery stick, cut into 1 cm cubes
1/2 cup (80 g) fresh or frozen
shelled peas
1 egg, lightly beaten

1 To make the pastry, sift the flour and 1/4 teaspoon salt into a large bowl. Add the butter and rub it into the flour with your fingertips until the mixture resembles fine breadcrumbs. Stir in the chopped herbs. Make a well, add almost all the water and mix with a flat-bladed knife until the mixture comes together in beads, adding a little more water if necessary.
2 Gently gather the dough together and lift it out onto a lightly floured work surface. Press together into a ball. Flatten slightly into a disc, wrap in plastic wrap and refrigerate for at least 20 minutes.

3 Preheat the oven to moderate 180°C (350°F/Gas 4). Place the chicken, lemon, 4 of the spring onions, bay leaves, chicken stock, wine, 1 1/2 cups (375 ml) water and 1/2 teaspoon salt into a large saucepan. Bring to the boil over high heat. Reduce the heat and simmer for 20 minutes, or until the chicken is cooked. Remove the chicken from the liquid and set aside. Return the liquid to the heat, bring to the boil for 10 minutes, or until it has reduced to 2 cups (500 ml), then strain into a bowl and set aside. Roughly cut the chicken into small pieces.
4 Melt the butter in a large saucepan over medium heat. When it is sizzling, add the onion and cook for 2–3 minutes, or until soft. Add the tarragon and mushrooms and cook, stirring occasionally, for 3–4 minutes, or until the mushrooms are soft. Add the flour and cook for 3 minutes, stirring the flour well. Pour in the reserved poaching liquid, bring to the boil and cook, stirring often, for 2 minutes, or until slightly thickened. Remove from the heat, then stir in the carrot, celery, peas and chicken. Divide the filling evenly among six 10 cm, 1 1/2 cup (375 ml) ramekins.
5 Divide the dough into six even portions. Roll out each portion into a flat disc, 12 cm in diameter (or use a 12 cm round cutter if you want smooth edges). Moisten the ramekin rims and cover with pastry rounds, pressing down firmly to seal the edges. Re-roll any pastry scraps and cut into shapes to decorate the tops. Prick with a fork, then brush with the egg. Bake for about 30 minutes, or until golden.

NUTRITION PER PIE
Protein 28 g; Fat 25 g; Carbohydrate 35.5 g; Dietary Fibre 4 g; Cholesterol 154 mg; 1990 kJ (475 cal)

Roughly cut the poached chicken breasts into small pieces.

Stir the carrot, celery, peas and chicken into the thickened mixture.

Roll out each portion of dough to a 12 cm flat disc.

Cover the filling with the pastry rounds, pressing down firmly to seal the edges.

WHITE FISH AND BROAD BEAN PIE

Preparation time: 30 minutes
+ 20 minutes refrigeration
+ 15 minutes standing
Cooking time: 1 hour 10 minutes
Serves 6

60 g butter
700 g firm white-fleshed fish fillets
    such as ling, hake or gemfish
350 g shelled broad beans
1 baby fennel bulb, thick outer
    leaves removed, thinly sliced
1 leek, thinly sliced
¼ cup (30 g) plain flour
1½ cups (375 ml) milk
100 g Cheddar, grated
pinch of ground nutmeg
¼ teaspoon cayenne pepper
2 tablespoons chopped fresh
    flat-leaf parsley
375 g home-made or bought
    shortcrust pastry (see page 6)
1 egg, lightly beaten

1 Melt half the butter in a large frying pan over meduim heat and cook the fish for 3–4 minutes each side, or until opaque. Cool, then discard any bones and skin. Flake the flesh into chunks.
2 Cook the beans in a saucepan of boiling water for 2 minutes. Drain, cool slightly, then remove the skins.
3 Melt the remaining butter in the pan. Add the fennel and leek and cook for 3–4 minutes, or until soft. Stir in the flour for 1 minute, then gradually pour in the milk. Stir over medium heat until the sauce is thick and smooth. Add the cheese, nutmeg, cayenne and salt and pepper and stir until the cheese melts. Fold in the fish, beans and parsley. Refrigerate until required.
4 Grease a 1.5 litre oval ovenproof dish. Roll two-thirds of the pastry large enough for the pie lid. Roll the scraps and remaining pastry to the same size. Cover with a tea towel and refrigerate for 20 minutes. Preheat the oven to moderately hot 190°C (375°F/Gas 5) and heat a baking tray.

5 Spoon the filling into the dish and level the surface. Top with the pastry lid. Trim and crimp the edges with a fork. Brush with egg. Cut the other sheet of pastry into a fish almost as long and wide as the pie. Lift onto the pie. Using scraps, make a mouth, eye and fins. Mark the tail with a knife and use the tip of a teaspoon to score scales. Brush with egg, then bake on the hot tray on the centre shelf for 45 minutes, covering with foil after 30 minutes. Cool in the dish for 15 minutes before serving.

NUTRITION PER SERVE
Protein 40 g; Fat 36 g; Carbohydrate 35 g; Dietary Fibre 6 g; Cholesterol 167 mg; 2600 kJ (620 cal)

Use a sharp knife to mark the tail of the pastry fish.

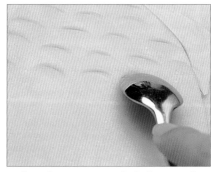

Make indentations over the body using the tip of a teaspoon.

CARBONADE PIE

Preparation time: 30 minutes
+ cooling
Cooking time: 3 hours 10 minutes
Serves 6

¼ cup (60 ml) olive oil
1 kg topside or chuck steak, cut into
    2 cm cubes
2 large onions, halved and thinly sliced
¼ cup (30 g) plain flour
1 tablespoon tomato paste
1½ cups (375 ml) beer
2 bay leaves
1 tablespoon soft brown sugar
2 cups (500 ml) beef stock
30 g butter
2 tablespoons plain flour, extra
600 g home-made or bought
    shortcrust pastry (see page 6)
1 egg, lightly beaten

1 Heat 2 tablespoons of the oil in
a large, heavy-based flameproof
casserole dish with a lid. Brown the
beef in batches over high heat for
3–4 minutes. Remove.
2 Reduce the heat to low, add the
remaining oil and the onion to the
pan and cook, stirring occasionally,
for 10 minutes, or until the onion is
soft and golden. Add the flour and
cook for 1 minute. Stir in the tomato
paste, beer, bay leaves and sugar.
Increase the heat to high and bring
to the boil. Add the stock and return
to the boil, then stir in the meat and
any juices. Reduce the heat, cover
and simmer, stirring occasionally, for
2 hours, or until the sauce is reduced
and the meat is tender. Remove from
the heat and cool slightly.
3 Preheat the oven to hot 210°C
(415°F/Gas 6–7). Lightly grease a
23 cm (top) 18 cm (base) 4 cm
(deep) pie dish. Heat a baking tray
in the oven. Remove the meat and
onion from the liquid and discard the
bay leaves. Pour the gravy into a jug.
Melt the butter in the same dish over
low heat. Stir in the extra flour and
cook for 1 minute, or until pale and
foaming. Increase the heat to medium
and slowly add the gravy, stirring
constantly for 3–4 minutes, or until
the sauce boils and thickens. Return
the meat and onion and season. Cool.
4 Set aside one third of the pastry.
Roll the other portion between two
sheets of baking paper until large
enough to line the base and side of
the pie dish. Line the dish, spoon in
the filling and smooth the surface.
Brush the pastry edges with egg. Roll
out the remaining pastry between
two sheets of baking paper until large
enough to cover the pie. Place over
the filling, seal the edges with a fork
and pierce the top. Trim the edges,
and decorate the pie if you wish.
Lightly brush with the egg, place the
dish on the hot tray and bake for
35–40 minutes, or until golden.
Allow to cool briefly before serving.

NUTRITION PER SERVE
Protein 44.5 g; Fat 44.5 g; Carbohydrate
55 g; Dietary Fibre 3 g; Cholesterol
182.5 mg; 3390 kJ (810 cal)

*Simmer until the sauce is reduced and the
meat is tender.*

ROASTED VEGETABLE AND FETA PIES

Preparation time: 30 minutes + cooling
Cooking time: 45 minutes
Makes 6

3 zucchini, cut into 1.5 cm rounds
½ small butternut pumpkin (420 g), cut into 2 cm cubes
1 red onion, cut into thin wedges
18 cap mushrooms, stalks removed
6 Roma tomatoes, quartered lengthways
1 tablespoon roughly chopped fresh oregano
2 teaspoons roughly chopped fresh rosemary
3 cloves garlic, crushed
2 tablespoons olive oil
6 sheets frozen ready-rolled shortcrust pastry, thawed
1 egg white, lightly beaten
200 g feta, cut into 1 cm cubes
1 tablespoon balsamic vinegar
200 g ready-made tzatziki

1 Preheat the oven to hot 220°C (425°F/Gas 7). Toss the zucchini, pumpkin, onion, mushrooms, tomatoes, herbs, garlic and oil together in a bowl, then bake in a large roasting dish for 20–30 minutes.

Remove the vegetables from the oven and allow to cool.
2 Using a plate as a guide, cut out six 22 cm rounds from the pastry and lightly brush each one all over with egg white. Arrange the vegetables and feta over each pastry circle, leaving a 4 cm border. Roughly tuck the pastry border in towards the filling. Brush the vegetables with balsamic vinegar.
3 Bake the pies for 10–15 minutes, or until puffed and golden. Serve with tzatziki.

NUTRITION PER PIE
Protein 22.5 g; Fat 64 g; Carbohydrate 82.5 g; Dietary Fibre 7.5 g; Cholesterol 78 mg; 4135 kJ (990 cal)

Bake the zucchini, pumpkin, onion, mushrooms, tomatoes, herbs and garlic.

Using a plate as a guide, cut out six rounds from the pastry.

Roughly tuck the pastry in towards the vegetable filling.

LAMB AND EGGPLANT PIE

Preparation time: 20 minutes
  + 30 minutes cooling
Cooking time: 1 hour 45 minutes
Serves 8–10

2 eggplants, cut into 2.5 cm cubes
¼ cup (60 ml) olive oil
3 onions, finely chopped
3 cloves garlic, chopped
1 teaspoon paprika
½ teaspoon ground cinnamon
¼ teaspoon ground nutmeg
650 g lamb mince
¼ cup (60 g) tomato paste
1 cup (250 ml) dry red wine
425 g can crushed tomatoes
1 cup (250 ml) beef stock
200 g Greek-style natural yoghurt
2 eggs, lightly beaten
200 g feta, crumbled
11 sheets filo pastry
olive oil spray

1 Preheat the oven to moderately hot 200°C (400°F/Gas 6) and grease a baking tray. Toss the eggplant with 2 tablespoons olive oil and place on the tray. Bake for 30 minutes, or until tender and brown. Remove, drain off any excess oil and set aside.

2 Meanwhile, heat the remaining oil in a large, deep frying pan over medium heat and cook the onion for 5 minutes, or until soft. Add the garlic and spices and cook for another minute.

3 Increase the heat to high, add the mince and cook for 5 minutes, or until brown. Add the tomato paste and cook for 2 minutes. Pour in the wine and cook for 3 minutes, stirring occasionally. Add the tomato and stock, bring to the boil, then reduce the heat and simmer for 30 minutes, or until the liquid has evaporated. Stir in the eggplant, then set aside for 30 minutes to cool completely.

4 Increase the oven to hot 220°C (425°F/Gas 7). Lightly grease a 2 litre pie dish. Combine the yoghurt, eggs and feta in a bowl.

5 Layer 6 sheets of filo in the base and sides of the pie dish, spraying the top of each sheet with olive oil. Top with all the lamb mixture, then pour in the yoghurt and feta mixture. Fold the overhanging pastry over the top of the filling, then top with another 5 filo sheets, spraying each sheet, to cover completely.

6 Bake on the lowest shelf for 30 minutes, then cook on the middle shelf for another 20–30 minutes, or until the pastry is crisp and golden.

NUTRITION PER SERVE (10)
Protein 22.5 g; Fat 17.5 g; Carbohydrate 14.5 g; Dietary Fibre 2.5 g; Cholesterol 98 mg; 1340 kJ (320 cal)

Spoon the lamb and eggplant mixture into the pie dish.

Pour the yoghurt and feta mixture over the lamb and eggplant mixture.

CREAMY MUSHROOM PIE

Preparation time: 45 minutes
+ 15 minutes soaking
+ 20 minutes refrigeration
+ cooling
Cooking time: 1 hour 5 minutes
Serves 4–6

Pastry
2 cups (250 g) plain flour
1/2 cup (75 g) fine polenta
125 g butter, chilled and cubed
1/4 cup (60 ml) cream
2–3 tablespoons iced water

10 g dried porcini mushrooms
150 g oyster mushrooms
1 large leek
150 g butter
2 large cloves garlic, crushed
200 g shiitake mushrooms,
    thickly sliced
200 g Swiss brown mushrooms,
    thickly sliced
350 g field mushrooms, sliced
100 g enoki mushrooms
2 tablespoons plain flour
1/2 cup (125 ml) dry white wine
1/2 cup (125 ml) vegetable or
    chicken stock
1/4 cup (60 ml) thick cream
2 tablespoons chopped fresh thyme
1 egg, lightly beaten

1 To make the pastry, sift the flour into a large bowl, then stir in the polenta and 1/2 teaspoon of salt. Add the butter and rub into the dry ingredients with your fingertips until the mixture resembles fine breadcrumbs. Make a well in the centre, pour in the cream and mix with a flat-bladed knife, using a cutting action, until the mixture comes together in beads. Add a little water if the mixture is too dry.
2 Gently gather the dough together and lift out onto a lightly floured work surface. Press together into a ball and then flatten slightly into a disc. Wrap in plastic wrap and refrigerate for 20 minutes.
3 Soak the porcini mushrooms in 1/4 cup (60 ml) boiling water for

about 15 minutes. Cut any large oyster mushrooms into halves. Thoroughly wash the leek and thinly slice it.
4 Preheat the oven to hot 210°C (415°F/Gas 6–7). Heat a baking tray in the oven. Lightly grease a 23 cm (top) 18 cm (base) 3 cm (deep) pie dish.
5 Drain the porcini mushrooms, reserving the soaking liquid, then coarsely chop the porcini mushrooms. Heat the butter in a large, deep frying pan over medium heat and cook the leek and garlic for 7–8 minutes, or until the leek is soft and golden. Add all the mushrooms to the pan and cook, stirring, for 5–6 minutes, or until the mushrooms are soft.
6 Add the flour to the pan and stir for 1 minute. Pour in the wine and reserved mushroom soaking liquid and bring to the boil for 1 minute, then pour in the stock and cook for 4–5 minutes, or until the liquid has reduced. Stir in the cream and cook for 1–2 minutes, or until thickened. Stir in the thyme and season. Cool.
7 Divide the pastry into two portions. Roll out one portion between two sheets of baking paper to 2 mm thick to line the base and side of the pie dish. Line the pie dish, then spoon in the cooled mushroom filling. Lightly brush the edges of the pastry with egg.
8 Roll out the remaining pastry between the baking paper until about 2 mm thick and cover the pie. Pinch the edges together and pierce the top three times with a fork. Trim the edges. Roll the trimmings and cut into mushroom shapes. Arrange over the pie and lightly brush the top with more egg. Place on the hot tray and bake for 35–40 minutes, or until the pastry is golden brown. Set aside for 5 minutes before slicing.

NUTRITION PER SERVE (6)
Protein 13.5 g; Fat 48 g; Carbohydrate 50.5 g; Dietary Fibre 7.5 g; Cholesterol 172.5 mg; 2900 kJ (695 cal)

Mix in the cream, using a cutting action, until the mixture comes together in beads.

Add all of the mushrooms to the pan and cook them until they are soft.

Spoon the cooled mushroom filling into the pastry-lined dish.

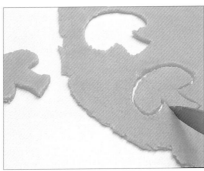

Cut the pastry trimmings into mushroom shapes to decorate the pie.

STEAK AND KIDNEY PIE

Preparation time: 40 minutes + cooling
Cooking time: 3 hours 10 minutes
Serves 6

½ cup (60 g) plain flour, seasoned
1.5 kg chuck steak, cut into
    2 cm cubes
1 ox kidney (500 g), cut into
    2 cm cubes
2 tablespoons olive oil
2 onions, chopped
125 g button mushrooms,
    quartered
40 g butter
1 cup (250 ml) beef or veal stock
¾ cup (185 ml) stout
2 tablespoons Worcestershire
    sauce
1 tablespoon anchovy essence
1 tablespoon chopped fresh
    flat-leaf parsley
600 g (1 quantity) quick flaky
    pastry (see page 9)
1 egg, lightly beaten

1 Place the flour in a bowl. Toss the steak and kidney pieces through the flour and shake off any excess.
2 Heat the oil in a large saucepan over medium heat, add the onion and cook for 5 minutes, or until soft and golden. Add the mushrooms and cook for another 5 minutes. Remove the onion and mushrooms from the pan.
3 Melt a third of the butter in the saucepan, add a third of the beef and kidney and cook over medium heat, turning occasionally, for 5 minutes, or until brown. Remove and repeat with the remaining butter, beef and kidney. Return all the meat to the saucepan, add the stock and stout, stir and bring slowly to boil. Reduce the heat and simmer for 2 hours, or until the meat is tender. Remove from the heat and allow the meat to cool.
4 Add the onion and mushrooms, Worcestershire sauce, anchovy essence and parsley to the meat.
5 Preheat the oven to moderate 180°C (350°F/Gas 4). Place the cooled filling into a 25 cm (top)

20 cm (base) 4 cm (deep) ceramic pie dish. Roll out the pastry between two sheets of baking paper to a round to fit the top of the pie dish. Moisten the rim of the dish with milk and place the pastry over the filling. Press firmly into place and brush with egg. Roll any scraps to decorate the top, brush with egg and bake for 40–45 minutes, or until golden.

NUTRITION PER SERVE
Protein 75.5 g; Fat 49.5 g; Carbohydrate 55 g; Dietary Fibre 3.5 g; Cholesterol 483.5 mg; 4100 kJ (980 cal)

Cook the beef and kidney in three batches until browned.

EGG AND BACON PIE

Preparation time: 20 minutes
+ 30 minutes refrigeration + cooling
Cooking time: 50 minutes
Serves 4–6

Pastry
450 g plain flour
125 g butter, chilled and cubed
250 g mascarpone

1 tablespoon olive oil
300 g bacon, diced
2 onions, halved and thinly sliced
1 tablespoon chopped fresh
   flat-leaf parsley
6 eggs
1 egg yolk

1 Sift the flour into a large bowl and rub in the butter with your fingertips until the mixture resembles fine breadcrumbs. Add the mascarpone and mix with a flat-bladed knife, using a cutting action, until the mixture begins to form lumps which leave the side of the bowl.
2 Turn the dough out onto a lightly floured surface and gently gather into a smooth ball. Flatten slightly into a disc, then cover in plastic wrap and refrigerate for 30 minutes.
3 Preheat the oven to warm 170°C (325°F/Gas 3). Lightly grease a 23 cm (top) 18 cm (base) 3 cm (deep) metal pie dish. Place a baking tray in the oven to preheat. Heat the oil in a frying pan and cook the bacon and onion over medium heat, stirring occasionally, for 5–7 minutes, or until just browning. Stir in the parsley. Set aside to cool.
4 Divide the pastry into two portions, one slightly larger than the other. Roll out the larger portion between two sheets of baking paper until large enough to line the base and side of the pie dish. Line the pie dish. Place the onion and bacon in the pastry shell and make six well-spaced holes in the mixture with the back of a spoon. Crack an egg into each of the holes. Brush the rim of the pastry with water. Roll out the remaining pastry between the baking paper until large enough to cover the top of the pie. Lift it onto the pie. Trim the excess pastry and seal the edges well. Re-roll the trimmings and make leaves to decorate the pie. Brush with egg yolk and bake on the hot tray for 40 minutes. Cover if it browns too quickly. Leave for 10 minutes before serving.

NUTRITION PER SERVE (6)
Protein 29.5 g; Fat 43.5 g; Carbohydrate 58.5 g; Dietary Fibre 3.5 g; Cholesterol 332 mg; 3085 kJ (735 cal)

Add the mascarpone and mix with a flat-bladed knife until lumps start to form.

Crack an egg into each hole in the onion and bacon filling mixture.

POTATO AND CHEESE PIE

Preparation time: 40 minutes
  + 20 minutes cooling
Cooking time: 1 hour 35 minutes
Serves 6–8

1 cup (250 ml) cream
1 bay leaf
1 kg waxy potatoes (e.g. desiree),
  thinly sliced
1 teaspoon chopped fresh chives
1 teaspoon chopped fresh thyme
500 g home-made or bought puff
  pastry (see page 8)
1 clove garlic, finely chopped
1 cup (125 g) grated Cheddar
1 egg, lightly beaten

1 Grease a 23 cm (top) 18 cm (base) 3 cm (deep) metal pie dish. Pour the cream into a large saucepan. Add the bay leaf, 1/4 teaspoon salt and some black pepper. Bring the cream to the boil very slowly over low heat and when it comes to the boil, remove it from the heat.
2 Add the potato slices to the cream mixture and stir well so that they are covered in the cream. Return the saucepan to high heat until the cream comes back to the boil. Reduce the

heat and simmer for 10 minutes, stirring occasionally. Remove the bay leaf. Fold in the herbs and set aside to cool for at least 20 minutes.
3 Preheat the oven to moderately hot 200°C (400°F/Gas 6). Divide the pastry into two portions. Roll out one portion between two sheets of baking paper until it is a circle large enough to fit the base and side of the dish. Line the pie dish with the pastry. Lay half the potato slices in the pie, sprinkle with the chopped garlic and half the cheese and season. Add the remaining potato slices and season again. Top with the remaining cheese.
4 Roll out the remaining portion of dough between two pieces of baking paper to a circle large enough to cover the top of the pie tin. Brush the

rim of the bottom piece of pastry with the beaten egg and cover with the pastry. Trim the edges. Make a small hole in the centre of the pastry. Re-roll the pastry scraps and cut into shapes with which to decorate the pie. Brush the pie with beaten egg and bake for 10 minutes.
5 Reduce the oven to moderate 180°C (350°F/Gas 4) and bake for about 1 hour 5 minutes. Cover the pie with foil halfway through baking if the pastry begins to brown. Insert a skewer through the hole in the pie to test if the potatoes are tender.

NUTRITION PER SERVE (8)
Protein 11.5 g; Fat 33 g; Carbohydrate 38.5 g; Dietary Fibre 2.5 g; Cholesterol 95.5 mg; 2085 kJ (500 cal)

Gently fold the fresh herbs into the creamy potato slices.

Sprinkle the remaining grated Cheddar over the potato slices.

MEDITERRANEAN PIE

Preparation time: 25 minutes
  + 20 minutes refrigeration
Cooking time: 35 minutes
Serves 4

Pastry
3 cups (375 g) plain flour
1 egg, lightly beaten
½ cup (125 ml) buttermilk
100 ml olive oil

2 tablespoons olive oil
100 g button mushrooms, sliced
400 g can whole peeled tomatoes,
    drained and roughly chopped
100 g sliced salami
170 g jar artichokes, drained
4 tablespoons fresh basil leaves, torn
⅔ cup (100 g) grated mozzarella
¼ cup (25 g) grated Parmesan
milk, to brush

1 Preheat the oven to hot 210°C (415°F/Gas 6–7). Grease a large baking tray and place in the oven to heat up. Sift the flour into a large bowl and add the egg and buttermilk.

Add the oil and mix with a large metal spoon until the mixture comes together and forms a soft dough. You may need to add a little water if the mixture is too dry. Turn onto a lightly floured surface and gather together into a smooth ball. Cover with plastic wrap and refrigerate for 20 minutes.
2 Heat the oil in a large frying pan, add the button mushrooms and cook over medium heat for 5 minutes, or until they have softened and browned a little.
3 Divide the pastry in half and roll each portion, between two sheets of baking paper, into a 30 cm round. Layer the chopped tomato, salami,

mushrooms, artichokes, basil leaves, mozzarella and Parmesan on one of the pastry rounds, leaving a 2 cm border. Season with salt and cracked black pepper.
4 Brush the border with milk. Top with the remaining pastry circle to enclose the filling, then pinch and seal the edges together. Make three slits in the top. Brush the top with milk. Place on the preheated tray and bake for 30 minutes, or until golden.

NUTRITION PER SERVE
Protein 29.5 g; Fat 51.5 g; Carbohydrate 75 g; Dietary Fibre 6.5 g; Cholesterol 94.5 mg; 3675 kJ (880 cal)

Gently gather the dough together into a smooth ball.

Brush the border of the pastry round with a little milk.

RAISED PORK PIES

Preparation time: 1 hour + cooling
Cooking time: 4 hours 35 minutes
Makes 6

Jelly
2 pig's trotters
1 onion, quartered
1 carrot, roughly chopped
1 celery stick, chopped
2 bay leaves
6 black peppercorns

Filling
250 g streaky bacon, diced
250 g pork spare ribs
500 g boned shoulder of pork, diced
1/2 teaspoon freshly grated nutmeg
2 teaspoons chopped fresh sage
2 teaspoons chopped fresh
    flat-leaf parsley
2 tablespoons brandy
2 drops anchovy essence

Pastry
675 g plain flour
175 g lard
1 egg, lightly beaten

1 To make the jelly, place all the ingredients and 1.75 litres water in a large saucepan and simmer for 3 hours, skimming off any scum. Strain, return the liquid to the pan and reduce until you have 2 cups (500 ml). Refrigerate until needed.
2 Meanwhile, to make the filling, put the bacon in a large bowl. Remove the meat from the spare ribs and cut into dice. Add to the bacon with the remaining filling ingredients and mix well. Season.
3 To make the pastry, sift the flour and 1/2 teaspoon salt into a large bowl and make a well. Bring 1 1/3 cups (350 ml) water and the lard to the boil in a saucepan. Pour into the flour and mix with a large wooden spoon to form a dough. Transfer to a lightly floured work surface and form into a ball. Working quickly, divide the dough into six portions and keep warm by covering with foil and placing in a warm place if necessary.

4 Take the first portion of dough and remove a quarter for the lid. Roll out the large portion to a thickness of 3–4 mm. Shape the warm dough around a greased and well floured up-turned 1 cup (250 ml) jar—the jar can also be wrapped in baking paper so the pastry can be more easily slipped off. Wrap the pastry in baking paper the same height as the jar and secure with string. Leave the pastry to cool a little. Turn upside down and remove the jar without damaging the pastry. Repeat with the remaining pastry to make six pastry cases. Cool slightly. Preheat the oven to moderate 180°C (350°F/Gas 4).
5 Divide the filling among the pastry cases. Roll out each reserved pastry portion to 3–4 mm thick to fit as lids. Brush the edges with beaten egg and attach the lids by pinching the edges together. You need to work quickly because if the dough cools down too much it will lose its elasticity.
6 Heat a baking tray. Make a hole in the centre of the lids 1 cm in diameter and decorate the pies with any remaining scraps of pastry. Brush the tops of the pies with beaten egg.
7 Bake the pies on the hot tray for 1 hour 20 minutes—cover the tops of the pies with foil after about 45 minutes to prevent them from colouring too much. Remove from the oven and allow to cool for about 25 minutes. Remove the baking paper and brush the tops and sides of the pies with beaten egg. Return to the oven and cook for 10–15 minutes, or until nicely coloured and firm to the touch. Remove and allow to cool.
8 Warm the jelly to a pouring consistency and gently pour the liquid jelly into the top of the pies until full. Chill for 2–3 hours, or until the jelly is set. Return the pies to room temperature for serving.

NUTRITION PER PIE
Protein 42 g; Fat 47 g; Carbohydrate 84.5 g; Dietary Fibre 4.5 g; Cholesterol 142.5 mg; 3940 kJ (940 cal)

COOK'S FILE
Note: It is important to keep the dough warm while working with it.

After 3 hours, strain the jelly and return the liquid to the saucepan.

Pour in the boiling water and lard and mix with a wooden spoon to form a dough.

Divide the pork mixture evenly among the pastry shells.

Attach the lids by pinching the pastry edges together.

SAUSAGE AND ONION PIE

Preparation time: 30 minutes
Cooking time: 55 minutes
Serves 6–8

1 tablespoon olive oil
2 onions, chopped
1 clove garlic, chopped
1 kg English-style pork sausages
1 tablespoon chopped fresh chives
1 teaspoon chopped fresh
   flat-leaf parsley
1½ teaspoons English mustard
1 egg, lightly beaten
600 g home-made or bought
   shortcrust pastry (see page 6)
1 egg, lightly beaten, extra

1 Preheat the oven to moderately hot 200°C (400°F/Gas 6) and grease a 23 cm (top) 18 cm (base) 3 cm (deep) metal pie dish. Heat the oil in a frying pan over medium heat, add the onion and garlic and cook for 5 minutes, or until soft and lightly golden. Transfer to a large bowl.
2 Remove the sausage meat from the casings, crumble slightly and add to the onion. Add the chives, parsley and mustard. Season well with salt and cracked black pepper. Mix well, then stir in the beaten egg.
3 Roll out two-thirds of the pastry between two sheets of baking paper to make a round large enough to fit the base and side of the pie tin. Line the tin with the pastry and trim the edges. Fill with the sausage mixture.
4 Roll out the remaining dough between two pieces of baking paper to a round large enough to cover the pie. Brush the rim of the first piece of pastry with the extra egg, then cover the top with the pastry and press the edges to seal. Make a small hole in the centre. Re-roll the scraps, cut into shapes and decorate the pie. Brush the pie with beaten egg and bake for 10 minutes. Reduce the oven to moderate 180°C (350°F/Gas 4) and bake for 40 minutes. Serve hot.

NUTRITION PER SERVE (8)
Protein 21.5 g; Fat 50.5 g; Carbohydrate 36.5 g; Dietary Fibre 3.5 g; Cholesterol 147.5 mg; 2835 kJ (680 cal)

COOK'S FILE
Note: It's important to use lean, English-style pork sausages as they contain grains which soak up any excess liquid. Other sausages will make the pie too wet.

Using your fingers, remove the sausage meat from the casings.

Fill the pastry-lined pie dish with the sausage mixture.

PRAWN POT PIES

Preparation time: 30 minutes
Cooking time: 40 minutes
Makes 4

2 tablespoons peanut oil
5 cm x 5 cm piece fresh ginger,
    peeled and grated
3 cloves garlic, chopped
1.5 kg raw medium prawns, peeled
    and deveined
¼ cup (60 ml) sweet chilli sauce
⅓ cup (80 ml) lime juice
1½ teaspoons fish sauce
⅓ cup (80 ml) cream
4 tablespoons chopped fresh
    coriander leaves
375 g home-made or bought
    shortcrust pastry (see page 6)
1 egg, lightly beaten
milk, for brushing

1 Preheat the oven to moderately hot 200°C (400°F/Gas 6). Grease a baking tray and put it in the oven to heat up. Heat the peanut oil in a large frying pan or wok over medium–high heat and stir-fry the ginger, garlic and prawns for 2–3 minutes. Remove the prawns from the pan. Add the chilli sauce, lime juice, fish sauce and cream and simmer over medium heat for about 5 minutes, or until the sauce has reduced by about one-third. Return the prawns to the pan and stir in the coriander leaves.
2 Roll out the pastry between two sheets of baking paper to 3 mm thick, and cut out four circles large enough to cover the tops of four 1¹/2 cup (375 ml) ramekins. Divide the filling among the ramekins, moisten the rims with milk and attach the lids. Cut a steam hole in each lid. Brush with the egg. Bake for 30 minutes, or until the pastry is lightly browned.

NUTRITION PER PIE
Protein 85 g; Fat 46 g; Carbohydrate 42.5 g; Dietary Fibre 3 g; Cholesterol 657 mg; 3870 kJ (925 cal)

Simmer the mixture until it has thickened and reduced by about one-third.

Add the prawns and chopped coriander to the mixture.

Cover the tops of the ramekins with the pastry rounds.

FAMILY-STYLE MEAT PIE

Preparation time: 30 minutes
+ cooling
+ 20 minutes refrigeration
Cooking time: 1 hour 45 minutes
Serves 6

1 tablespoon oil
1 onion, chopped
1 clove garlic, crushed
750 g beef mince
1 cup (250 ml) beef stock
1 cup (250 ml) beer
1 tablespoon tomato paste
1 tablespoon vegetable yeast extract
1 tablespoon Worcestershire sauce
2 teaspoons cornflour
375 g home-made or bought
    shortcrust pastry (see page 6)
375 g home-made or bought puff
    pastry (see page 8)
1 egg, lightly beaten

1 Heat the oil in a large saucepan over medium heat, add the onion and cook for 5 minutes, or until golden. Increase the heat to high, add the garlic and mince and cook, breaking up any lumps, for about 5 minutes, or until the mince changes colour.
2 Add the stock, beer, tomato paste, yeast extract, Worcestershire sauce and ½ cup (125 ml) water. Reduce the heat to medium and cook for 1 hour, or until there is little liquid left. Combine the cornflour with 1 tablespoon water, then stir into the mince and cook for 5 minutes, or until thick and glossy. Remove from the heat and cool completely.
3 Lightly grease a 23 cm (top) 18 cm (base) 3 cm (deep) pie tin. Roll the shortcrust pastry out between two sheets of baking paper until large enough to line the base and side of the tin. Remove the top sheet of paper and invert the pastry into the tin, then remove the remaining sheet of paper. Use a small ball of pastry to help press the pastry into the tin, allowing any excess to hang over.
4 Roll out the puff pastry between two sheets of baking paper to a 24 cm circle. Spoon the filling into the pastry shell and smooth it down. Brush the pastry edges with beaten egg, then place the puff pastry over the top. Cut off any overhang with a sharp knife. Press the top and bottom pastries together, then scallop the edges with a fork or your fingers, and refrigerate for 20 minutes. Preheat the oven to moderately hot 200°C (400°F/Gas 6) and heat a baking tray.
5 Brush the remaining egg over the top of the pie, place on the hot tray on the bottom shelf of the oven (this helps make a crisp crust for this pie) and bake for 25–30 minutes, or until golden and well puffed

NUTRITION PER SERVE
Protein 38 g; Fat 43.5 g; Carbohydrate 52 g; Dietary Fibre 2.5 g; Cholesterol 129.5 mg; 3120 kJ (745 cal)

Spoon the cooled meat filling into the pastry shell.

Trim the edges of the puff pastry with a sharp knife.

PUMPKIN, LEEK AND CORN PIE

Preparation time: 30 minutes
+ cooling
Cooking time: 1 hour 15 minutes
Serves 6

1/3 cup (80 ml) olive oil
2 leeks, thinly sliced
2 large cloves garlic, chopped
1 butternut pumpkin (1.7 kg), peeled, seeded and cut into 1 cm cubes
3 corn cobs
1 1/2 cups (185 g) grated Cheddar
1 teaspoon chopped fresh rosemary
1/2 cup (15 g) chopped fresh flat-leaf parsley
12 sheets filo pastry
5 eggs, lightly beaten

1 Preheat the oven to moderate 180°C (350°F/Gas 4). Grease a 32 cm x 24 cm, 6 cm deep, ovenproof dish.
2 Heat 1 tablespoon of the oil in a small saucepan and cook the leek and garlic over medium heat for 10 minutes, stirring occasionally, until soft and lightly golden. Transfer to a large bowl and allow to cool.
3 Meanwhile, cook the pumpkin in boiling water for 5 minutes, or until just tender. Drain well and cool. Cook the corn in a large saucepan of boiling water for 7–8 minutes, or until tender. Drain, leave until cool enough to handle, then cut away the kernels. Add these to the bowl with the pumpkin, cheese, rosemary and parsley, season generously and mix gently but thoroughly.
4 Place the filo pastry on a clean workbench and cover with a damp tea towel to prevent the pastry drying out. Lightly brush one sheet of filo with oil and place in the dish. Layer five more sheets in the dish, brushing all but the last sheet with oil.
5 Gently stir the eggs into the pumpkin mixture, then spoon into the dish. Cover with the remaining filo pastry, again brushing each layer with oil, and tuck in the edges. Bake for 1 hour, or until the pastry is golden brown and the filling has set. Serve immediately.

NUTRITION PER SERVE
Protein 22 g; Fat 29 g; Carbohydrate 37.5 g; Dietary Fibre 6 g; Cholesterol 180.5 mg; 2080 kJ (495 cal)

Spoon the pumpkin and corn mixture into the ovenproof dish.

Tuck the edges of the filo pastry into the side of the dish.

ROSEMARY LAMB COBBLER

Preparation time: 30 minutes
Cooking time: 2 hours
Serves 4–6

600 g boned lamb leg, cut into
   2 cm chunks
¼ cup (30 g) plain flour, well
   seasoned with salt and pepper
20 g butter
2 tablespoons olive oil
8 spring onions, chopped
3 cloves garlic, crushed
2 cups (500 ml) beef stock
1 cup (250 ml) dry white wine
2 teaspoons wholegrain mustard
2 teaspoons finely chopped
   fresh rosemary
2 celery sticks, sliced
1 teaspoon grated lemon rind
1 teaspoon lemon juice
½ cup (125 g) sour cream

Cobbler topping

¾ cup (185 ml) milk
1 egg
40 g butter, melted
1½ cups (185 g) plain flour
2 teaspoons baking powder
1 teaspoon finely chopped
   fresh rosemary
2 tablespoons finely chopped
   fresh flat-leaf parsley

1 Put the lamb pieces and flour in a plastic bag and shake well to evenly coat the lamb. Shake off any excess.
2 Heat the butter and 1 tablespoon of the olive oil in a large saucepan over high heat, then cook half the lamb for 5 minutes, or until well browned. Remove from the pan. Add the remaining oil if needed and cook the remaining lamb.
3 Add half the spring onion to the pan with the garlic and cook for 30 seconds, or until the spring onion is softened. Return the lamb to the pan with the stock, wine, mustard, rosemary, celery, lemon rind and juice and bring to the boil. Reduce the heat and simmer, stirring occasionally, for 1¼ hours, or until the lamb is tender and the sauce has thickened.
4 Remove from the heat and stir a little of the sauce into the sour cream, then stir it all back into the lamb mixture with the remaining spring onion. Leave to cool while you make the topping.
5 Preheat the oven to moderately hot 190°C (375°F/Gas 5). To make the topping, combine the milk, egg and melted butter in a large bowl. Add the combined sifted flour and baking powder with the herbs, 1 teaspoon salt and some cracked black pepper and stir until you have a thick, sticky batter—you may need to add a little more flour if it is too wet, or milk if it is too dry.
6 Spoon the lamb into a deep 23 cm (top) 18 cm (base) 3.5 cm (deep) pie dish and, using two spoons, cover the top with small dollops of the batter, leaving a little gap between each dollop because the cobbler mix will spread. Cook for 30 minutes, or until the topping is risen and golden.

NUTRITION PER SERVE (6)
Protein 31 g; Fat 27.5 g; Carbohydrate 31 g; Dietary Fibre 2.5 g; Cholesterol 153 mg; 2180 kJ (520 cal)

Put the lamb and flour in a plastic bag and shake until the meat is lightly covered.

Cook the lamb in a large saucepan until it is nicely browned.

Simmer the mixture until the meat is tender and the sauce has thickened.

Stir a little of the meaty sauce into the sour cream.

Stir the batter thoroughly until it is thick and sticky.

Add spoonfuls of the batter to the top of the pie, leaving a small gap between each one.

CHINESE BARBECUED PORK PIES

Preparation time: 35 minutes
    + 1 hour refrigeration
Cooking time: 45 minutes
Makes 4

2 tablespoons cornflour
¼ cup (60 ml) oyster sauce
¼ cup (60 ml) rice wine
2 tablespoons kecap manis
2 tablespoons lime juice
1 tablespoon grated fresh ginger
½ teaspoon ground white pepper
400 g Chinese barbecued pork,
    cut into 1 cm dice
150 g snowpeas, sliced
2 cups (100 g) thinly sliced Chinese
    cabbage
375 g home-made or bought
    shortcrust pastry (see page 6)
375 g home-made or bought puff
    pastry (see page 8)
milk, for brushing
1 teaspoon sesame seeds

1 Preheat the oven to moderate 180°C (350°F/Gas 4). Grease four 11 cm (top) 9 cm (base) 3 cm (deep) metal pie dishes. Mix the cornflour with 2 tablespoons water. Heat a large frying pan over low heat and add the oyster sauce, rice wine, kecap manis, lime juice, ginger, white pepper and the cornflour mixture. Simmer for 2 minutes, or until very thick. Add the pork, snowpeas and cabbage. Cook, stirring, for 5 minutes. Cool, then refrigerate for 1 hour, or until cold.
2 Meanwhile, roll out the shortcrust pastry between two sheets of baking paper until it is 3 mm thick. Cut out four 16 cm rounds—you can use a saucer as a guide. Line the pie dishes with the pastry, then refrigerate.
3 When the filling is cold, fill the pastry shells. Roll out the puff pastry between the baking paper to 3 mm thick and cut out four rounds large enough to cover the tops of the pie dishes. Cover the pies with the puff pastry rounds and trim any excess. Use a fork to seal the edges and prick a few holes in the top. Brush the lids with milk, sprinkle with sesame seeds, and bake for 35 minutes, or until golden.

NUTRITION PER PIE
Protein 35 g; Fat 60.5 g; Carbohydrate 86 g; Dietary Fibre 7 g; Cholesterol 112.5 mg; 4360 kJ (1040 cal)

Add the pork, snow peas and cabbage and cook, stirring, for 5 minutes.

Cut four 16 cm rounds of shortcrust pastry and use them to line the pie dishes.

Cut rounds from the puff pastry and cover the tops of the pies.

COTTAGE PIE

Preparation time: 30 minutes
Cooking time: 1 hour 30 minutes
Serves 6–8

2 tablespoons olive oil
2 onions, chopped
2 carrots, diced
1 celery stick, diced
1 kg beef mince
2 tablespoons plain flour
1½ cups (375 ml) beef stock
1 tablespoon soy sauce
1 tablespoon Worcestershire sauce
2 tablespoons tomato sauce
1 tablespoon tomato paste
2 bay leaves
2 teaspoons chopped fresh flat-leaf
    parsley

Topping
800 g potatoes, cut into 2 cm cubes
400 g parsnips, cut into 2 cm cubes
30 g butter
½ cup (125 ml) milk

1 Heat the oil in a large frying pan over medium heat and cook the onion, carrot and celery, stirring occasionally, for 5 minutes, or until the onion has softened and is lightly coloured. Add the mince and cook for 7 minutes, then stir in the flour and cook for 2 minutes. Add the stock, soy sauce, Worcestershire sauce, tomato sauce, tomato paste, and the bay leaves and simmer over low heat for 30 minutes, stirring occasionally. Remove from the heat and leave to cool while you make the topping. Remove the bay leaves and stir in the parsley.

2 To make the topping, place the potato and parsnip in a large saucepan with ½ teaspoon salt, cover with water, bring to the boil and cook over medium heat for 15–20 minutes, or until softened and cooked through. Drain, return to the pan and add the butter. Mash with a potato masher or push through a coarse sieve. Fold in enough of the milk to make a firm mash.

3 Preheat the oven to moderate 180°C (350°F/Gas 4) and lightly grease a 2.5 litre ovenproof dish. Spoon the filling into the dish and spread the topping over it. Fluff it up with a fork. Bake for 25 minutes, or until the topping is golden.

NUTRITION PER SERVE (8)
Protein 30.5 g; Fat 18 g; Carbohydrate 26.5 g; Dietary Fibre 4 g; Cholesterol 78 mg; 1640 kJ (390 cal)

Mash the potato and parsnip together with a potato masher.

Spoon the cooled meat filling into the ovenproof dish.

MINI OYSTER PIES

Preparation time: 30 minutes
  + 20 minutes cooling
Cooking time: 45 minutes
Makes 30

2 cups (500 ml) fish stock
1 tablespoon olive oil
2 leeks, chopped
30 g butter
1 tablespoon plain flour
1 teaspoon lemon juice
1 teaspoon chopped fresh chives
8 sheets frozen puff pastry, thawed
30 fresh oysters
1 egg, lightly beaten

1 Pour the stock into a saucepan and simmer over medium heat for 15 minutes, or until reduced by half —you will need 1 cup (250 ml).
2 Heat the oil in a saucepan over medium heat. Add the leek and cook, stirring well, for 5 minutes, or until soft and lightly coloured. Transfer to a small bowl to cool slightly.
3 Melt the butter in a small saucepan over low heat. Add the flour and cook, stirring well, for 2 minutes, or until the flour is golden. Remove from the heat and gradually add the fish stock, stirring well. Return to the heat and bring to the boil, stirring constantly for 2 minutes, or until the mixture has thickened. Add the lemon juice, chives and leek and season well with salt and cracked black pepper. Set aside to cool for 20 minutes. Preheat the oven to moderately hot 200°C (400°F/Gas 6) and grease two baking trays.
4 Using a 6 cm round cutter, cut out thirty circles of pastry and put 1 oyster and a heaped teaspoon of the filling on top of each, leaving a 5 mm border. Lightly brush the edges with beaten egg.
5 Cut thirty 8 cm circles from the remaining sheets of pastry. Cover the filling with these rounds and press the edges with a fork to seal. Brush the tops with the remaining beaten egg, place on the baking trays and bake for 15–20 minutes, or until golden and well puffed.

NUTRITION PER PIE
Protein 3.5 g; Fat 12 g; Carbohydrate 16.5 g; Dietary Fibre 1 g; Cholesterol 24 mg; 785 kJ (190 cal)

Gradually add the fish stock and boil, stirring constantly, until thickened.

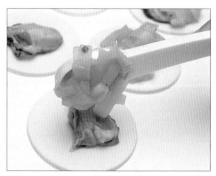

Place an oyster and a heaped teaspoon of filling on each pastry round.

CHICKEN, POTATO AND PRESERVED LEMON PIE

Preparation time: 40 minutes
+ 20 minutes refrigeration + cooling
Cooking time: 1 hour 15 minutes
Serves 4–6

2 tablespoons olive oil
2 leeks, thinly sliced
3/4 preserved lemon, pulp removed, rind washed and cut into thin strips
1 kg chicken thigh fillets, cut into bite-size pieces
2 tablespoons plain flour
1 cup (250 ml) chicken stock
250 g kipfler potatoes, thinly sliced
2 tablespoons chopped fresh flat-leaf parsley
1 egg, lightly beaten

Pastry
100 g self-raising flour
150 g plain flour
60 g butter, chilled and cubed
60 g lard, chilled and cubed
3–4 tablespoons iced water
1 egg, lightly beaten

1 Heat the oil in a large frying pan, add the leek and cook over medium heat for 2–3 minutes, or until golden. Add the preserved lemon and cook for 3 minutes, or until the lemon is fragrant. Remove from the pan.
2 Add a little extra oil to the pan if needed, add the chicken in batches and cook, stirring, for 5 minutes, or until browned. Return all the chicken to the pan along with the leek and lemon. Sprinkle with flour and cook, stirring, for 2 minutes, or until the flour is mixed through.
3 Gradually stir in the chicken stock, then add the potato. Bring to the boil, then reduce the heat and simmer for 7 minutes, or until thickened slightly. Stir in the parsley. Transfer to a bowl and allow to cool completely.
4 To make the pastry, sift the flours and a pinch of salt into a large bowl and rub in the chopped butter and lard with your fingertips until the mixture resembles fine breadcrumbs. Make a well, add almost all the water and mix with a flat-bladed knife, using a cutting action, until the mixture comes together in beads, adding more water if necessary.
5 Turn out the dough onto a lightly floured surface, gather into a ball, cover in plastic wrap and refrigerate for 20 minutes. Preheat the oven to moderately hot 200°C (400°F/Gas 6).

Heat a baking tray in the oven.
6 Spoon the filling into a 26 cm (top) 16 cm (base) 4 cm (deep) pie plate. Roll out the dough between two sheets of baking paper until large enough to cover the pie. Remove the top sheet and invert the pastry onto the pie, allowing any excess to hang over the sides. Use a small sharp knife, trim any excess pastry, then press to seal on the rim. Cut a few steam holes in the top and decorate the pie with any remaining pastry. Brush with the egg, place on the hot tray and bake for 35–40 minutes, or until the crust is crisp and golden.

NUTRITION PER SERVE (6)
Protein 40 g; Fat 39 g; Carbohydrate 40 g; Dietary Fibre 3.5 g; Cholesterol 240 mg; 2795 kJ (665 cal)

When the chicken mixture has thickened slightly, stir in the parsley.

63

Pie decoration

Decorations such as a simple fork-pressed edge or an impressive lattice top add to the appeal of pies. Follow our guidance as shown below or just use your creative skills to make a work of art.

Traditionally, savoury pies were decorated whereas sweet pies were not. This was in order to differentiate the two when both were served at the same table. However, we now decorate simply for effect. As well as giving pies a finished touch, decorating can be very practical. Not only can you use up excess pastry trimmings but decorating helps seal the edges of a double-crusted (pastry base and top) pie so that the lid remains securely in place.

DECORATIVE EDGES

Fork-pressed Press a lightly floured fork around the edge of the pie crust.
Fluted Press the pastry between your thumb and forefinger for a rippled effect.
Scalloped Press an upturned teaspoon on the pastry edges to mark semicircles.
Checkerboard Make cuts in the pastry edge. Bend every second square inward.
Petal-edged Flute the pastry edge,

then press the tines of a fork lightly into the centre of each flute — first in one direction, then in the other.
Leaves Cut out leaf shapes with a cutter or the point of a sharp knife and mark veins using the back of a knife. Attach to the lip of the pie using a little water or egg glaze.
Plait Cut three long strips of pastry about 5 mm wide. Plait them together and attach to the lip of the pie using a little water or egg, pressing gently.

Crimped Press the pastry between the thumb and forefinger, while indenting with the other forefinger.
Rope Twist two long sausages of pastry together and attach to the edge with a little water or egg.
Feathering Lift the pastry off the lip of the dish so that it stands upright, then snip diagonally into the edge of the pie. Push one point inwards and one outwards.

DECORATIVE TOPS

There are endless shapes and forms you can use to decorate pies, from cherries and stars to abstract patterns, or simple initials. Alternatively, you can buy small biscuit cutters in various shapes. When rolling out pastry trimmings, don't make the shapes too thick or they won't cook through. To attach them, first brush the pie lid with egg glaze, then arrange the decorations on top and glaze them as well.

For the opposite effect, you can cut out shapes from the pastry lid so that there are attractive windows into the filling underneath.

Another impressive finish for a pie is a lattice top. Roll the pastry out on a sheet of baking paper to a square a little larger than the pie. Using a fluted pastry wheel or a small sharp knife, cut strips of pastry about 1.5 cm wide. On another sheet of baking paper, lay half the strips vertically, 1 cm apart. Fold back alternate strips of pastry and lay a strip of pastry horizontally across the unfolded strips, then fold the vertical strips back into place. Next, fold the lower strips back and lay another piece horizontally. Repeat with all the strips. Refrigerate until firm, then invert the lattice onto the pie and remove the baking paper. Press the edges to seal, then trim off the excess pastry.

You can vary not only the width of the pastry strips but also the spacing, to create a tightly woven lattice or one with just three or four strips.

Alternatively, you can make life simple and buy a lattice cutter. Just roll out the pastry and roll over it with the cutter. Gently open the lattice out, lift it onto your pie and then trim the edges.

Clockwise from top left: Crimped edge; Plaited edge with leaves to decorate top; Fluted edge with cut out shapes on top

SPICED CHINESE ROAST DUCK PIES

Preparation time: 50 minutes
+ 30 minutes refrigeration
+ cooling
Cooking time:1 hour
Makes 4

Pastry
2 cups (250 g) plain flour
2 teaspoons baking powder
50 g lard, chilled and grated

1/3 cup (80 ml) vegetable oil
1 tablespoon plus 1 teaspoon
    sesame oil
1 clove garlic, finely chopped
2 teaspoons finely chopped
    fresh ginger
150 g oyster mushrooms, sliced
1 Chinese roast duck (from Chinese
    barbecue shops), meat shredded
    into 2–3 cm lengths
3 spring onions, cut into 3 cm lengths
    plus 4 spring onions, finely sliced
1 teaspoon sugar
1 teaspoon finely ground Sichuan
    pepper
1/4 cup (30 g) plain flour
1/4 cup (60 ml) Chinese rice wine
1 1/2 cups (375 ml) chicken stock
1 tablespoon light soy sauce

1 Sift the flour, baking powder and 1 teaspoon salt into a bowl. Mix the lard into the flour with your fingertips until the mixture resembles fine breadcrumbs. Make a well and gradually pour in 3/4 cup (185 ml) boiling water. Use a wooden spoon to combine the flour and water by gradually stirring the flour into the centre of the bowl until the dough comes together.
2 Gather the dough into a ball, wrap in plastic wrap and refrigerate for 30 minutes.
3 Heat 2 tablespoons vegetable oil and 1 teaspoon sesame oil in a frying pan over medium heat. Add the garlic and ginger and cook for 2 minutes, then add the mushrooms, duck meat, 3 cm lengths of spring onion, sugar, Sichuan pepper and a pinch of salt

and cook for 3–4 minutes. Add the flour and cook for 2 minutes, stirring well. Pour in the rice wine, stir again, then add the stock and soy sauce. Bring to the boil and cook, stirring for 2–3 minutes, or until the mixture thickens. Remove from the heat and set aside to cool.
4 Preheat the oven to moderate 180°C (350°F/Gas 4). Grease four 11 cm (top) 6 cm (base) 2 cm (deep) pie tins. Roll the pastry into a log, then roughly divide it into eight pieces. Combine the remaining vegetable and sesame oils in a small bowl. Roll each piece of dough into a flat 10 cm round, brush with some of the oil mixture and sprinkle with the sliced spring onion. Roll the discs into small logs, then coil each log into a cake.
5 Roll out four of the dough cakes into flat 16 cm discs. Use to line the

pie tins, then fill the pastry cases with the duck filling. Roll the remaining pastry into 15 cm circles and use as lids. Press with a fork to seal. Brush with some of the oil mixture and bake for 40–45 minutes, until golden.

NUTRITION PER PIE
Protein 29.5 g; Fat 45.5 g; Carbohydrate 55.5 g; Dietary Fibre 5 g; Cholesterol 120 mg; 3175 kJ (760 cal)

Fill the pastry-lined tins with the cooled duck filling.

HAM, CHEESE AND POTATO PIE

Preparation time: 25 minutes
    + cooling + 10 minutes standing
Cooking time: 1 hour 45 minutes
Serves 6–8

¼ cup (60 ml) olive oil
3 onions, finely chopped
1 clove garlic, finely chopped
300 g ham, chopped
430 g desiree potatoes, diced
2 cups (250 g) grated Cheddar
2 eggs
⅓ cup (80 ml) cream
2 teaspoons chopped fresh chives
4 sheets ready-rolled frozen
    puff pastry, thawed
1 egg, lightly beaten

1 Heat the oil in a large frying pan over medium heat. Add the onion and garlic and cook, stirring occasionally, for 5 minutes, or until the onion softens. Add the ham and potato and cook, stirring occasionally, for 5–7 minutes, or until the potatoes soften slightly.

Transfer to a large bowl and stir in the Cheddar.
2 Mix together the eggs and cream and pour into the bowl. Add the chives and mix thoroughly. Season well with salt and cracked black pepper. Allow to cool.
3 Preheat the oven to moderately hot 200°C (400°F/Gas 6). Grease a 23 cm (top) 18 cm (base) 3 cm (deep) pie dish. Line the pie dish with 2 sheets of puff pastry, and brush the edge with beaten egg. Spoon the filling into the pie dish.
4 Cut the remaining sheets of pastry into quarters, and each quarter into three equal lengths. Place the strips,

overlapping, around the top of the pie, leaving the centre open. Press down the edges so that the top and bottom layers stick together, then trim the edges with a sharp knife.
5 Brush the top of the pie with the beaten egg, and bake in the oven for 30 minutes. Reduce the temperature to moderate 180°C (350°F/Gas 4) and cook the pie for another hour, covering the top with foil if it is browning too much. Leave for 10 minutes before serving.

NUTRITION PER SERVE (8)
Protein 24 g; Fat 44 g; Carbohydrate 39 g; Dietary Fibre 2.5 g; Cholesterol 153 mg; 2700 kJ (645 cal)

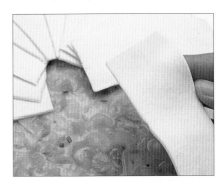

Pour the creamy egg mixture into the bowl with the ham and cheese.

Overlap the pastry strips around the pie, leaving a gap in the middle.

ITALIAN EASTER PIE

Preparation time: 40 minutes
    + 20 minutes cooling
Cooking time: 1 hour 5 minutes
Serves 6–8

450 g silverbeet, stalks removed
1 cup (80 g) fresh white breadcrumbs
1 cup (250 ml) milk
550 g ricotta (see Note)
2 cups (200 g) coarsely grated
    Parmesan
8 eggs
pinch of ground nutmeg
pinch of cayenne pepper
10 small fresh marjoram leaves
150 g butter
20 sheets filo pastry

1 Bring 2 cups (500 ml) salted water to the boil in a large saucepan. Add the silverbeet, cover and cook, stirring occasionally, for 5 minutes, or until wilted. Drain well. When cool enough to handle, wring out all the liquid in a clean tea towel. Chop well.

2 Preheat the oven to moderate 180°C (350°F/Gas 4). In a large bowl, put the breadcrumbs and milk, leave for 5 minutes, then add the ricotta, half the Parmesan, 4 eggs, the nutmeg, cayenne, marjoram and the chopped silverbeet. Season well and mix.

3 Melt the butter, then lightly brush a 23 cm springform tin with it. Line the base and the side with a sheet of filo pastry. Brush with melted butter and place another filo sheet on top, positioned so that any exposed wall of the tin is covered. Continue in this way, using a total of ten sheets of filo. Don't worry about the filo forming folds on the tin walls, just push them flat as you brush with butter.

4 Spoon the filling into the tin. Make four deep indentations in the surface around the edge of the pie, then break an egg into each. Season and sprinkle with the remaining Parmesan. Fold over any overhanging pastry. Cover with the remaining filo, buttering each layer.

5 Bake for 40 minutes, cover the top with foil, then bake for another 20 minutes. Cool in the tin for 20 minutes. Serve warm or at room temperature.

NUTRITION PER SERVE (8)
Protein 28.5 g; Fat 37.5 g; Carbohydrate 29 g; Dietary Fibre 3 g; Cholesterol 285.5 mg; 2360 kJ (565 cal)

COOK'S FILE
Note: Use ricotta from a wheel, not pre-packaged ricotta as this tends to be very moist.

Gently break an egg into each of the four indentations you have made.

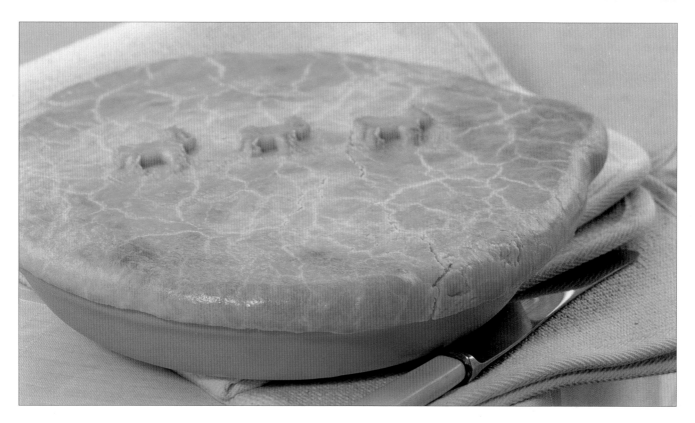

CHUNKY VEAL AND CAPSICUM PIE

Preparation time: 40 minutes
    + 10 minutes resting + cooling
Cooking time: 2 hours
Serves 6

1/3 cup (80 ml) olive oil
3 capsicums, cored, seeded and cut
    into 2.5 cm pieces
2 cloves garlic, crushed
1 kg neck, shoulder or breast of veal,
    trimmed and cut into 2.5 cm pieces
1/4 cup (30 g) plain flour, seasoned
40 g butter
2 onions, finely chopped
8 French shallots, peeled
1/4 teaspoon cayenne pepper
2 teaspoons red wine vinegar
3/4 cup (185 ml) chicken stock
2 tablespoons chopped fresh flat-leaf
    parsley
375 g home-made or bought
    shortcrust pastry (see page 6)
1 egg, lightly beaten

1 Heat half the oil in a large saucepan. Sauté the capsicum over medium heat for 2–3 minutes. Add the garlic, cover the pan and reduce the heat to low. Cook gently for 5 minutes, then remove from the pan.
2 Put the veal and flour in a plastic bag and shake until the veal is evenly coated, shaking off any excess. Heat the butter and the remaining oil over high heat in the same saucepan and cook the veal in batches until evenly browned. Return all the veal to the pan, add the onion, shallots and cayenne and reduce the heat to low. Cook, covered, for 10 minutes. Stir in the vinegar, cover and turn off the heat. Leave for 10 minutes.
3 Add the capsicum, stock and parsley to the meat, bring to the boil, then reduce the heat to low. Cover and simmer for 20 minutes, or until the meat is tender.
4 Uncover and cook for another 30–40 minutes to reduce the liquid until it thickens and darkens. Season to taste and cool slightly. Preheat the oven to moderately hot 200°C (400°F/Gas 6) and preheat a baking tray. Lightly grease a 23 cm (top) 18 cm (bottom) 3 cm (deep) pie dish.
5 Spoon the filling into the pie dish, levelling the surface. Roll the dough out between two sheets of baking paper to a size slightly larger than the top of the pie dish. Carefully cover the filling and press the pastry over the edge to seal. Neatly trim the edges with a sharp knife. Brush the surface with egg.
6 Roll out the pastry scraps and cut out three cows using a biscuit cutter. Arrange on the pie surface and brush with egg. With the point of a knife, make cuts at the front and back feet of the cows to resemble grass. Place on the hot tray and bake for 30 minutes, or until golden.

NUTRITION PER SERVE
Protein 44 g; Fat 36.5 g; Carbohydrate 33 g; Dietary Fibre 2.5 g; Cholesterol 201 mg; 2660 kJ (635 cal)

Spoon the filling into the pie dish, then level the surface.

KANGAROO AND JUNIPER BERRY PIES

Preparation time: 30 minutes
+ cooling
+ 30 minutes refrigeration
Cooking time: 3 hours 10 minutes
Makes 6

¼ cup (60 ml) olive oil
2 cloves garlic, crushed
150 g streaky bacon, diced
800 g kangaroo rump, cut into
    1.5 cm pieces (see Variation)
¼ cup (30 g) plain flour
½ cup (125 ml) dry red wine
1 teaspoon dried juniper berries,
    ground
3 bay leaves
1 tablespoon fresh thyme, chopped
2 teaspoons grated orange rind
2 cups (500 ml) beef stock
200 g small pickling onions, trimmed
1 egg, lightly beaten
sour cream, to serve

Pastry

450 g plain flour
300 g frozen lard (see Note)
150 ml iced water

1 Heat 1 tablespoon of the oil in a large flameproof casserole dish and cook the garlic and bacon over low heat for 4–5 minutes, or until softened but not browned. Remove from the dish with a slotted spoon.
2 Add the remaining oil to the pan and increase the heat to high. Cook the kangaroo meat in batches for 3 minutes, or until lightly browned. Return all the meat to the pan and sprinkle with the flour, stirring to combine.
3 Pour the wine into the pan and cook, stirring constantly, scraping the base and side, for 2–3 minutes, or until nearly all of the wine has evaporated. Return the garlic and bacon to the pan along with the ground juniper berries, bay leaves, thyme, orange rind and beef stock. Add enough water to cover the meat and bring to the boil, then reduce the heat and simmer, covered, for 1 hour.

4 Add the onions to the casserole dish and cook for another 45–60 minutes, or until the meat is tender, stirring occasionally and adding a little water if the mixture begins to catch on the base of the pan. Season, to taste, with salt and pepper. Remove from the heat and allow to cool. Remove the bay leaves.
5 Preheat the oven to moderately hot 200°C (400°F/Gas 6). While the meat is cooling, make the pastry. Sift the flour and ¼ teaspoon salt into a large bowl and grate the frozen lard onto the flour using the largest grating side. Rub the lard into the flour with your fingertips until the mixture resembles coarse breadcrumbs. Add the water 1 tablespoon at a time until the dough just comes together, being careful not to overwork the dough. Shape into a ball and flatten slightly. Cover with plastic wrap and refrigerate for at least 30 minutes.
6 On a lightly floured surface, roll out two-thirds of the pastry and cut out six circles large enough to line the base and sides of six pie tins 12.5 cm (top) 9.5 cm (base) 3 cm (deep). Line the pie tins with the pastry. Divide the filling among the tins and roll out the remaining pastry to make six lids. Brush the rims of the pastry lining with beaten egg, then place the lids on top, pinching to seal. Trim the edges and brush the tops with beaten egg. Make small steam holes on the tops of the pies.
7 Bake for 20 minutes, then reduce the temperature to moderate 180°C (350°F/Gas 4) and cook for another 25–30 minutes, or until the pastry is crisp and golden. Serve with sour cream on the side.

NUTRITION PER PIE
Protein 42.5 g; Fat 64 g; Carbohydrate 52 g; Dietary Fibre 3.5 g; Cholesterol 158.5 mg; 4025 kJ (960 cal)

COOK'S FILE
Note: It is important that the lard is frozen so it is easy to grate into the flour.
Variation: Any other red meat can be used instead of kangaroo meat.

Pour the wine into the pan and cook until it has nearly evaporated.

Remove the casserole dish from the heat and discard the bay leaves.

Roll out the remaining pastry to make six lids for the pies.

Brush the edge of the pastry with egg, then place the lids on top, pinching to seal.

BEEF AND CARAMELISED ONION PIE

Preparation time: 40 minutes
+ 20 minutes cooling
Cooking time: 2 hours 20 minutes
Serves 6–8

1/3 cup (80 ml) oil
2 large red onions, thinly sliced
1 teaspoon dark brown sugar
1 kg lean rump steak, cut into
    2 cm cubes
1/4 cup (30 g) plain flour, seasoned
2 cloves garlic, crushed
225 g button mushrooms, sliced
1 cup (250 ml) beef stock
150 ml stout
1 tablespoon tomato paste
1 tablespoon Worcestershire sauce
1 tablespoon chopped fresh thyme
350 g potatoes, cut into 1.5 cm
    pieces
2 carrots, cut into 1.5 cm pieces
600 g quick flaky pastry (see page 9)
1 egg, lightly beaten

1 Heat 2 tablespoons of the oil in a frying pan over medium heat and cook the onion for 5 minutes, or until light brown, then add the sugar and cook for 7–8 minutes, or until the onion caramelises. Remove from the pan. Wipe the pan clean.

2 Toss the beef in flour and shake off the excess. Heat the remaining oil in the same pan and cook the meat in batches over high heat until browned. Return all the meat to the pan, add the garlic and mushrooms and cook for 2 minutes. Add the stock, stout, tomato paste, Worcestershire sauce and thyme. Bring to the boil, then reduce the heat and simmer, covered, for 1 hour. Add the potato and carrot and simmer for 30 minutes. Remove from the heat and allow to cool.

3 Preheat the oven to moderately hot 190°C (375°F/Gas 5). Grease a 1.25 litre pie dish. Pour in the filling, then top with the onion. Roll the pastry out between two sheets of baking paper until it is 3 cm wider than the pie dish. Cut a 2 cm strip around the edge of the pastry circle, brush with water and place damp-side-down on the rim of the dish. Cover with the remaining pastry, pressing down on the edges to join the two pastries. Knock up the edges by using the back of a knife to make small slashes in the edges of the pastry. Re-roll any pastry scraps and use them to decorate the pie. Brush with egg and bake for 25 minutes, or until golden.

NUTRITION PER SERVE (8)
Protein 36 g; Fat 32 g; Carbohydrate 46.5 g; Dietary Fibre 3.5 g; Cholesterol 112.5 mg; 2615 kJ (625 cal)

Spoon the caramelised onion over the filling in the pie dish.

Place the strip of pastry damp-side-down on the rim of the dish.

ITALIAN ZUCCHINI PIE

Preparation time: 30 minutes
  + 30 minutes refrigeration
  + 30 minutes draining
Cooking time: 55 minutes
Serves 6

Pastry
2½ cups (310 g) plain flour
⅓ cup (80 ml) olive oil
1 egg, beaten
3–4 tablespoons iced water

600 g zucchini
150 g provolone cheese, grated
120 g ricotta
3 eggs
2 cloves garlic, crushed
2 teaspoons finely chopped fresh basil
pinch of ground nutmeg
1 egg, lightly beaten

1 To make the pastry, sift the flour and ½ teaspoon salt into a large bowl and make a well. Combine the oil, egg and almost all the water and add to the flour. Mix with a flat-bladed knife, using a cutting action, until the mixture comes together in beads, adding a little more water if necessary. Gather into a ball, wrap in plastic wrap and refrigerate for 30 minutes.

2 Preheat the oven to moderately hot 200°C (400°F/Gas 6) and heat a baking tray. Grease a 23 cm (top) 18 cm (base) 3 cm (deep) pie dish. To make the filling, grate the zucchini and toss with ¼ teaspoon salt. Place in a colander for 30 minutes to drain. Squeeze out any excess liquid with your hands. Place in a large bowl and add the provolone, ricotta, eggs, garlic, basil and nutmeg. Season well and mix thoroughly.

3 Roll out two-thirds of the pastry between two sheets of baking paper until large enough to line the base and side of the dish. Remove the top sheet and invert into the dish.

4 Spoon the filling into the pastry shell and level the surface. Brush the exposed rim of the dough with egg. Roll out two-thirds of the remaining dough between the baking paper to make a lid. Cover the filling with it, pressing the edges together firmly. Trim the edges and reserve the scraps. Crimp the rim. Prick the top all over with a skewer and brush with egg.

5 Roll the remaining dough into a strip about 30 x 10 cm. Using a long sharp knife, cut this into nine lengths 1 cm wide. Press three ropes together at one end and press these onto the workbench to secure them. Plait the ropes. Make two more plaits with the remaining lengths. Trim the ends and space the plaits parallel across the centre of the pie. Brush with egg. Bake on the hot tray for 50 minutes, or until golden.

NUTRITION PER SERVE
Protein 20.5 g; Fat 26.5 g; Carbohydrate 40 g; Dietary Fibre 3.5 g; Cholesterol 184.5 mg; 2010 kJ (480 cal)

Spoon the filling into the pastry shell and level the surface.

INDIAN-STYLE SPICY LAMB AND APRICOT PIE

Preparation time: 40 minutes
+ 20 minutes refrigeration
+ cooling
Cooking time: 2 hours 45 minutes
Serves 8–10

Pastry
2¹⁄₂ cups (310 g) plain flour
160 g ghee, chilled and cut into
    small pieces
1 teaspoon cumin seeds
1 teaspoon sugar
¹⁄₄–¹⁄₂ cup (60–125 ml) iced water

1.4 kg boned lamb shoulder, cut into
    1.5 cm cubes
1 cup (250 g) natural yoghurt
2 teaspoons garam masala
1¹⁄₂ tablespoons grated fresh ginger
1 teaspoon chilli powder
2 teaspoons ghee
2 onions, sliced
3 cloves garlic, crushed
1 long fresh green chilli, finely
    chopped
6 cardamom pods, crushed
1 teaspoon ground coriander
2 teaspoons ground cumin
2 x 425 g cans crushed tomatoes
100 g dried apricots, halved, soaked
    in 1 cup (250 ml) warm water
¹⁄₂ cup (125 g) thick natural yoghurt
    (optional)

1 To make the pastry, sift the flour into a food processor and add the ghee, cumin seeds, sugar and 1 teaspoon salt. Process until the mixture resembles fine breadcrumbs, then gradually add the water until the pastry comes together in beads. Do not over-process. Gently gather the dough together into a ball, place on a lightly floured surface and press into a disc. Refrigerate for 20 minutes.

2 Combine the lamb, yoghurt, garam masala, ginger, chilli powder and ¹⁄₂ teaspoon salt in a large bowl.

3 Heat the ghee in a large saucepan, add the onion and cook over medium heat for 10 minutes, or until soft and golden. Add the garlic and fresh chilli and cook for 1 minute, then add the remaining spices and cook for another minute.

4 Add the lamb and yoghurt mixture to the pan and cook, stirring occasionally, until combined. Add the tomato, bring to the boil, reduce the heat and simmer for 1¹⁄₄ hours, then add the apricots and simmer for another 15 minutes, or until the lamb is tender. Set aside to cool.

5 Preheat the oven to hot 220°C (425°F/Gas 7). Preheat a baking tray. Grease a deep 23 cm fluted tart tin or pie dish. Roll out two thirds of the pastry between two sheets of baking paper to a size large enough to fit the tin. Remove the top sheet of paper and invert the pastry into the tin. Fill the pastry shell with the lamb curry. Brush the edges with a little water. Roll out the remaining pastry between the sheets of baking paper until large enough to cover the top of the pie dish. Position the lid on top of filling. Make two or three slits for the steam to escape, then trim the pastry edges.

6 Place the pie on the heated baking tray and bake on the lowest shelf for 30 minutes. Move to the centre shelf and bake for another 30 minutes, or until brown. Leave for 10 minutes before slicing. Serve with a dollop of yoghurt, if desired.

NUTRITION PER SERVE (10)
Protein 19 g; Fat 20.5 g; Carbohydrate 33.5 g; Dietary Fibre 4 g; Cholesterol 94 mg; 1660 kJ (395 cal)

COOK'S FILE
Note: Because of the ghee content in the pastry for this pie, it is very difficult to make successfully by hand. It is better to use a food processor as described in the recipe. The filling mixture may seem a little runny when ready to go in the pie, but once it is cooked the sauce thickens. Ask your butcher to bone the lamb shoulder for you.

Gently gather the dough together into a ball and place on a lightly floured surface.

Add the spices to the onion mixture and cook for another minute.

Spoon the lamb curry mixture into the pastry shell.

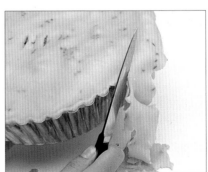

Make steam holes on top of the pie and trim the pastry edges with a sharp knife.

PUMPKIN AND FETA PIE

Preparation time: 30 minutes
+ cooling + 20 minutes
refrigeration
Cooking time: 1 hour 25 minutes
Serves 6

700 g butternut pumpkin, cut into
2 cm pieces
4 cloves garlic, unpeeled
5 tablespoons olive oil
2 small red onions, halved and sliced
1 tablespoon balsamic vinegar
1 tablespoon soft brown sugar
100 g good-quality feta, broken into
small pieces
1 tablespoon chopped fresh rosemary

Pastry
2 cups (250 g) plain flour
125 g butter, chilled and cubed
1/2 cup (50 g) grated Parmesan
3–4 tablespoons iced water

1 Preheat the oven to moderately
hot 200°C (400°F/Gas 6). Place the
pumpkin and garlic cloves on a
baking tray, drizzle with 2 tablespoons
oil and bake for 25–30 minutes, or
until the pumpkin is tender. Transfer
the pumpkin to a large bowl and the
garlic to a plate. Leave the pumpkin
to cool.

2 Meanwhile, heat 2 tablespoons oil
in a pan, add the onion and cook over
medium heat, stirring occasionally,
for 10 minutes. Add the vinegar and
sugar and cook for 15 minutes, or
until the onion is caramelised.
Remove from the heat and add to the
pumpkin. Cool completely.

3 While the vegetables are cooling,
make the pastry. Sift the flour and
1 teaspoon salt into a large bowl and
rub in the butter with your fingertips
until the mixture resembles fine
breadcrumbs. Stir in the Parmesan.
Make a well, add almost all the water
and mix with a flat-bladed knife,
using a cutting action, until the
mixture comes together in beads.
Add a little more water if needed to
bring the dough together.

4 Gather the dough together and lift
onto a lightly floured work surface.
Press together into a ball and flatten
slightly into a disc. Cover in plastic
wrap and refrigerate for 20 minutes.

5 Add the feta and rosemary to the
pumpkin. Squeeze out the garlic flesh
and mix it through the vegetables.
Season, to taste.

6 Roll out the dough between two
sheets of baking paper to a 35 cm
circle. Remove the top sheet of paper
and place the bottom paper with the
pastry on a tray. Arrange the pumpkin
and feta mixture on top, leaving a
6 cm border. Fold over the edges,
pleating as you fold, and bake for
30 minutes, or until crisp and golden.

NUTRITION PER SERVE
Protein 13.5 g; Fat 38.5 g; Carbohydrate
41.5 g; Dietary Fibre 3.5 g; Cholesterol
72.5 mg; 2360 kJ (565 cal)

*Fold the edges of the pastry over the
pumpkin and feta filling.*

RICH SNAPPER PIES

Preparation time: 20 minutes
Cooking time: 1 hour 20 minutes
Makes 4

2 tablespoons oil
4 onions, thinly sliced
¼ cup (30 g) plain flour
2 cups (500 ml) fish stock
½ cup (125 ml) dry white wine
2 cups (500 ml) cream
1 tablespoon chopped fresh
   chives
1 kg skinless snapper fillets,
   cut into 2.5 cm pieces
2 teaspoons truffle-flavoured oil
   (optional)
1 sheet ready-rolled puff pastry,
   thawed
1 egg, lightly beaten

1 Preheat the oven to hot 210°C (415°F/Gas 6–7). Heat the oil in a large frying pan, add the onion and cook, stirring occasionally, over medium heat for 20 minutes, or until the onion is golden brown and slightly caramelised. Add the flour and cook, stirring, for 1 minute.
2 Gradually add the fish stock and wine to the pan, stir thoroughly, then bring to the boil and cook for 5 minutes, or until thickened. Stir in the cream and bring back to the boil. Reduce the heat and simmer for about 20 minutes, or until the liquid is reduced by half and has thickened. Stir in the chives, then the fish.
3 Divide the mixture among four 1¾ cup (440 ml) ramekins. Add ½ teaspoon truffle oil to each pie.
4 Cut the pastry sheets into rounds slightly larger than the tops of the ramekins and press onto the ramekins. Brush lightly with the beaten egg and make a cut in the tops for steam to escape. Bake for 30 minutes, or until crisp, golden and puffed. Serve with crusty bread.

NUTRITION PER PIE
Protein 60.5 g; Fat 80 g; Carbohydrate 30.5 g; Dietary Fibre 2 g; Cholesterol 378 mg; 4595 kJ (1100 cal)

COOK'S FILE
Note: You can substitute bream, sea perch or a fleshy white fish for the snapper fillets.

Sprinkle the chives into the mixture, then stir through.

Place the pastry circle over the ramekin and press gently to seal.

CHEESE AND ONION PIE

Preparation time: 25 minutes
  + 10 minutes cooling
Cooking time: 45 minutes
Serves 4

2 tablespoons olive oil
2 onions, chopped
1½ cups (185 g) grated Cheddar
1 tablespoon chopped fresh flat-leaf
  parsley
1 teaspoon English mustard
2 teaspoons Worcestershire sauce
2 eggs, beaten
2 sheets frozen ready-rolled
  puff pastry, thawed

1 Preheat the oven to moderately hot 190°C (375°F/Gas 5). Heat the oil in a large frying pan over medium heat, add the onion and cook for 5–7 minutes, or until soft and golden. Transfer to a bowl and allow to cool for 10 minutes.
2 Add the cheese, parsley, mustard and Worcestershire sauce to the onion and mix well. Add half the egg to the bowl and season well with salt and cracked black pepper.
3 Cut each sheet of pastry into a 23 cm circle. Lay one sheet of pastry on a lined baking tray. Spread the filling over the pastry base, piling it higher in the middle and leaving a 2 cm border. Lightly brush the border with some of the beaten egg and place the second sheet on top, stretching it slightly to neatly fit the bottom. Press and seal the edges well and brush the top with the remaining beaten egg. Cut two slits in the top for steam to escape.
4 Bake for 10 minutes, then reduce the heat to moderate 180°C (350°F/ Gas 4) and cook for another 20–25 minutes, or until the pastry is risen, crisp and golden.

NUTRITION PER SERVE
Protein 20.5 g; Fat 46.5 g; Carbohydrate 33.5 g; Dietary Fibre 2 g; Cholesterol 158.0 mg; 2625 kJ (630 cal)

Mix the cheese, parsley, mustard and Worcestershire sauce through the onion.

Brush the border of the pastry with some of the beaten egg.

Lift the second pastry circle over the cheese and onion filling.

WELSH LAMB PIE

Preparation time: 20 minutes
+ cooling
Cooking time: 2 hours 35 minutes
Serves 6

750 g boned lamb shoulder, cubed
¾ cup (90 g) plain flour, seasoned
2 tablespoons olive oil
200 g bacon rashers, finely chopped
2 cloves garlic, chopped
4 large leeks, sliced
1 large carrot, chopped
2 large potatoes, cut into 1 cm cubes
1¼ cups (315 ml) beef stock
1 bay leaf
2 teaspoons chopped fresh flat-leaf
parsley
375 g quick flaky pastry (see page 9)
1 egg, lightly beaten

1 Toss the meat in the seasoned flour and shake off the excess. Heat the oil in a large frying pan over medium heat. Cook the meat in batches for 4–5 minutes, or until well browned, then remove from the pan. Add the bacon to the pan and cook for 3 minutes. Add the garlic and leek and cook for about 5 minutes, until the leek is soft.

2 Put the meat in a large saucepan, add the leek and bacon, carrot, potato, stock and bay leaf and bring to the boil, then reduce the heat, cover and simmer for 30 minutes. Uncover and simmer for 1 hour, or until the meat is cooked and the liquid has thickened. Season to taste. Remove the bay leaf, stir in the parsley and set aside to cool.

3 Preheat the oven to moderately hot 200°C (400°F/Gas 6). Place the filling into a 23 cm (top) 18 cm (base) x 3 cm (deep) pie dish. Roll out the pastry between two sheets of baking paper until large enough to cover the pie. Remove the top sheet of paper and invert over the filling.

4 Trim the edges and pinch to seal. Re-roll the scraps and cut out shapes to decorate the pie. Cut two slits in the top for steam to escape. Brush with egg and bake for 45 minutes, or until the pastry is crisp and golden.

NUTRITION PER SERVE
Protein 42 g; Fat 27.5 g; Carbohydrate 43 g; Dietary Fibre 4.5 g; Cholesterol 147 mg; 2465 kJ (590 cal)

Season the meat mixture and remove the bay leaf.

Cut out shapes from the pastry scraps to decorate the pie.

79

SWEET PIES

RHUBARB PIE

Preparation time: 40 minutes
+ 30 minutes refrigeration + cooling
Cooking time: 1 hour
Serves 6

Pastry
2 cups (250 g) plain flour
30 g unsalted butter, chilled and cubed
70 g Copha (white vegetable shortening), chilled and cubed
2 tablespoons icing sugar
160 ml iced water

1.5 kg rhubarb, trimmed and cut into 2 cm pieces
1 cup (250 g) caster sugar
1/2 teaspoon ground cinnamon
2 1/2 tablespoons cornflour
30 g unsalted butter, cubed
1 egg, lightly beaten
icing sugar, to dust

1 Grease a 25 cm (top) 20 cm (base) 4 cm (deep) ceramic pie dish. Sift the flour and 1/2 teaspoon salt into a large bowl and rub in the butter and Copha with your fingertips until the mixture resembles fine breadcrumbs. Stir in the icing sugar. Make a well, add almost all the water and mix with a flat-bladed knife, using a cutting action, until it comes together in beads. Add more water if necessary.
2 Gently gather the dough together and lift onto a lightly floured work surface. Press into a ball, flatten into a disc, cover in plastic wrap and refrigerate for 30 minutes.
3 Put the rhubarb, sugar, cinnamon and 2 tablespoons water in a saucepan and stir over low heat until the sugar is dissolved. Simmer, covered, for 5–8 minutes, stirring occasionally, until the rhubarb is tender. Mix the cornflour with 1/4 cup (60 ml) water and add to the pan. Bring to the boil, stirring until thickened. Allow to cool. Preheat the oven to moderate 180°C (350°F/Gas 4) and heat a baking tray.
4 Roll out two-thirds of the dough to a 30 cm circle and invert into the pie dish. Spoon the rhubarb into the dish. Dot with butter.
5 Roll out the remaining pastry to form a lid. Moisten the pie rim with egg and press the top in place. Trim the edges and make a slit in the top. Decorate, if desired, with pastry scraps. Brush with egg and bake on the hot tray for 35–40 minutes, or until golden. Dust with icing sugar.

NUTRITION PER SERVE
Protein 7.5 g; Fat 21.5 g; Carbohydrate 82 g; Dietary Fibre 6 g; Cholesterol 55 mg; 2290 kJ (545 cal)

Simmer the rhubarb mixture, stirring occasionally, until tender.

Moisten the rim of the pastry with egg and press the pastry top into place.

CHOCOLATE FUDGE PECAN PIE

Preparation time: 30 minutes
+ 40 minutes refrigeration + cooling
Cooking time: 1 hour 20 minutes
Serves 6

Pastry
1¼ cups (155 g) plain flour
2 tablespoons cocoa powder
2 tablespoons soft brown sugar
100 g unsalted butter, chilled and
    cubed
2–3 tablespoons iced water

2 cups (200 g) pecans, roughly
    chopped
100 g dark chocolate, chopped
½ cup (95 g) soft brown sugar
⅔ cup (170 ml) light or dark corn
    syrup
3 eggs, lightly beaten
2 teaspoons vanilla essence

1 Grease a 23 cm (top) 18 cm (base) 3 cm (deep) pie dish. Sift the flour, cocoa and sugar into a bowl and rub in the butter with your fingertips until the mixture resembles fine breadcrumbs. Make a well, add almost all the water and mix with a knife, adding more water if necessary.
2 Gather the dough together and lift onto a sheet of baking paper. Press into a disc and refrigerate for 20 minutes. Roll out the pastry between two sheets of baking paper to fit the dish. Line the dish and trim the edges. Refrigerate for 20 minutes.
3 Preheat the oven to moderate 180°C (350°F/Gas 4). Cover the pastry with crumpled baking paper and fill with baking beads or (uncooked) rice. Bake for 15 minutes, then remove the paper and beads and bake for another 15–20 minutes, or until the base is dry. Set aside to cool completely.
4 Place the pie dish on a flat baking tray to catch any drips if the filling bubbles over. Spread the pecans and chocolate over the pastry base. Combine the sugar, corn syrup, eggs and vanilla in a jug and whisk

together with a fork. Pour into the pastry shell, and bake for 45 minutes (the filling will still be a bit wobbly, but will set on cooling). Cool completely before cutting to serve.

NUTRITION PER SERVE
Protein 10.5 g; Fat 45.5 g; Carbohydrate 82.5 g; Dietary Fibre 4 g; Cholesterol 132 mg; 3240 kJ (775 cal)

Use a rolling pin to help line the pie dish with the pastry.

Combine the sugar, corn syrup, egg and vanilla and whisk with a fork.

MANGO AND PASSIONFRUIT PIES

Preparation time: 25 minutes
   + refrigeration
Cooking time: 25 minutes
Makes 6

750 g home-made or bought sweet
   shortcrust pastry (see page 7)
3 ripe mangoes (900 g), peeled and
   sliced or chopped, or 400 g can
   mango slices, drained
1/4 cup (60 g) passionfruit pulp
1 tablespoon custard powder
1/3 cup (90 g) caster sugar

1 egg, lightly beaten
icing sugar, to dust

1 Preheat the oven to moderately
hot 190°C (375°F/Gas 5). Grease six
10 cm (top) 8 cm (base) 3 cm (deep)
fluted flan tins or round pie dishes.
Roll out two-thirds of the pastry
between two sheets of baking paper
to a thickness of 3 mm. Cut out six
13 cm circles. Line the tins with the
circles and trim the edges. Refrigerate
while you make the filling.
2 Combine the mango, passionfruit,
custard powder and sugar in a bowl.
3 Roll out the remaining pastry
between two sheets of baking paper

to a thickness of 3 mm. Cut out six
11 cm circles. Re-roll the trimmings
and cut into shapes.
4 Fill the pastry cases with the
mango mixture and brush the edges
with egg. Top with the pastry circles
and press the edges to seal. Trim the
edges and decorate with the pastry
shapes. Brush the tops with beaten
egg and dust with icing sugar. Bake
for 20–25 minutes, or until the
pastry is golden brown. Delicious
served with cream.

NUTRITION PER PIE
Protein 11 g; Fat 29 g; Carbohydrate
85.5 g; Dietary Fibre 6 g; Cholesterol
113.5 mg; 2685 kJ (640 cal)

*Line the tins with the pastry circles and
trim the edges.*

*Carefully spoon the mango mixture into the
pastry cases.*

*Decorate the tops of the pies with shapes
cut from the pastry trimmings.*

PUMPKIN PIE

Preparation time: 20 minutes
+ 40 minutes refrigeration + cooling
Cooking time: 1 hour 30 minutes
Serves 6–8

Pastry

1¼ cups (155 g) plain flour
100 g unsalted butter, chilled
and cubed
2 teaspoons caster sugar
4 tablespoons iced water

750 g butternut pumpkin, cubed
2 eggs, lightly beaten
1 cup (185 g) soft brown sugar
⅓ cup (80 ml) cream
1 tablespoon sweet sherry or brandy
½ teaspoon ground ginger
½ teaspoon ground nutmeg
1 teaspoon ground cinnamon

1 Sift the flour into a large bowl and rub in the butter with your fingertips until the mixture resembles fine breadcrumbs. Mix in the caster sugar. Make a well in the centre, add almost all the water and mix with a flat-bladed knife, using a cutting action, until the mixture comes together in beads, adding more water if needed.
2 Gather the dough together and lift out onto a lightly floured work surface. Press into a ball and flatten slightly into a disc. Cover in plastic wrap and refrigerate for 20 minutes.
3 Roll out the pastry between two sheets of baking paper until it is large enough to cover the base and side of a 23 cm (top) 18 cm (base) 3 cm (deep) pie dish. Line the dish with pastry, trim away the excess and crimp the edges with a fork. Cover with plastic wrap and refrigerate for 20 minutes.
4 Preheat the oven to moderate 180°C (350°F/Gas 4). Cook the pumpkin in boiling water until tender. Drain, then mash with a potato masher. Push through a large sieve into a bowl. Allow to cool.
5 Line the pastry shell with a piece of crumpled baking paper large enough to cover the base and sides.

Pour in baking beads or uncooked rice and bake for 10 minutes, then remove the paper and beads and cook for another 10 minutes, or until lightly golden. Set aside to cool.
6 Whisk the eggs and sugar together in a large bowl. Add the cooled pumpkin, cream, sherry and the spices and stir thoroughly. Pour the mixture into the pastry shell, smooth

the surface and bake for 1 hour, or until set. If the pastry begins to brown too much during cooking, cover the edges with foil. Allow the pie to cool before serving with cream or ice cream.

NUTRITION PER SERVE (8)
Protein 6 g; Fat 16.5 g; Carbohydrate 45 g; Dietary Fibre 2 g; Cholesterol 90 mg; 1470 kJ (350 cal)

Bake the pastry for 10 minutes, then remove the paper and beads and cook until golden.

Stir the pumpkin, cream, sherry and spices into the egg and sugar mixture.

NUTTY FIG PIE

Preparation time: 40 minutes
+ 20 minutes refrigeration
Cooking time: 1 hour
Serves 8

375 g home-made or bought
shortcrust pastry (see page 6)
200 g hazelnuts
100 g pine nuts
100 g flaked almonds
100 g blanched almonds
150 ml cream
60 g unsalted butter
1/4 cup (90 g) honey
1/2 cup (95 g) soft brown sugar
150 g dessert figs, cut into quarters

1 Preheat the oven to moderately hot 200°C (400°F/Gas 6) and grease a 23 cm (top) 18 cm (base) 3 cm (deep) pie tin. Roll the pastry out between two sheets of baking paper until large enough to cover the base and side of the pie tin. Remove the top sheet and invert the pastry into the tin, allowing any excess to hang over. Trim with a sharp knife and prick the base several times with a fork. Score the edge with a fork. Refrigerate for 20 minutes, then bake for 15 minutes, or until crisp, dry and lightly golden. Allow to cool.
2 Meanwhile, bake the hazelnuts on a baking tray for 8 minutes, or until the skins start to peel away. Tip into a tea towel and rub to remove the skins. Place the pine nuts, flaked almonds and blanched almonds on a baking tray and bake for 5–6 minutes, or until lightly golden.
3 Place the cream, butter, honey and brown sugar in a saucepan and stir over medium heat until the sugar dissolves and the butter melts. Remove from the heat and stir in the nuts and figs. Spoon the mixture into the pastry case and bake for 30 minutes. Remove and cool until firm before slicing. Delicious served with chocolate ice cream.

NUTRITION PER SERVE
Protein 11.5 g; Fat 57.5 g; Carbohydrate 44 g; Dietary Fibre 5.5 g; Cholesterol 57.5 mg; 3030 kJ (725 cal)

Invert the pastry into the pie tin, allowing any excess to hang over the sides.

Use a small, sharp knife to trim the excess pastry from the edge.

Spoon the nut and fig mixture into the pastry-lined pie tin.

CHERRY PIE

Preparation time: 30 minutes
  + 1 hour refrigeration
Cooking time: 1 hour
Serves 6

500 g home-made or bought sweet
  shortcrust pastry (see page 6)
2 x 425 g cans seedless black
  cherries, drained well
1/3 cup (60 g) soft brown sugar
1 1/2 teaspoons ground cinnamon
1 teaspoon finely grated lemon rind
1 teaspoon finely grated orange rind
1–2 drops almond essence
1/4 cup (25 g) ground almonds
1 egg, lightly beaten

1 Preheat the oven to moderately hot 190°C (375°F/Gas 5). Roll out two-thirds of the dough between two sheets of baking paper to form a circle large enough to fit a 22 cm (top) 20 cm (base) 2 cm (deep) pie plate. Remove the top sheet of baking paper and invert the pastry into the pie plate. Cut away the excess pastry with a small sharp knife. Roll out the remaining pastry large enough to cover the pie. Refrigerate, covered in plastic wrap, for 20 minutes.

2 Place the cherries, sugar, cinnamon, rinds and almond essence in a bowl and mix to coat the cherries.

3 Line the pastry base with ground almonds. Spoon in the filling, brush the pastry edges with beaten egg, and cover with the pastry lid. Use a fork to seal the edges pastry. Cut four slits in the top of the pie to allow steam to escape, then brush the pastry with beaten egg. Bake for 1 hour, or until the pastry is golden and the juices are bubbling through the slits in the pastry. Serve warm.

NUTRITION PER SERVE
Protein 7.5 g; Fat 24.5 g; Carbohydrate 61.5 g; Dietary Fibre 4 g; Cholesterol 53.5 mg; 2055 kJ (490 cal)

Line the base of the pastry with a thin layer of ground almonds.

Spoon the cherry filling over the ground almonds in the pastry case.

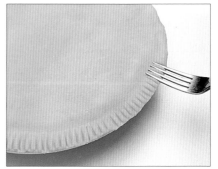

Cover the pie with the lid, then use a fork to seal the edges.

VANILLA AND CARAMEL SWIRL ICE CREAM PIE

Preparation time: 1 hour + 6 hours
   freezing + 20 minutes refrigeration
   + cooling
Cooking time: 20 minutes
Serves 6–8

250 g plain chocolate biscuits
150 g unsalted butter, melted
1 vanilla bean, split
1 cup (250 ml) milk
2 cups (500 ml) cream
2/3 cup (160 g) caster sugar
6 egg yolks

Caramel
1/2 cup (125 g) caster sugar
1/4 cup (60 ml) cream
30 g unsalted butter

1 Lightly grease a 27 cm (top) 15.5 cm (base) 4.5 cm (deep) pie dish. Finely crush the biscuits in a food processor. Stir in the butter and mix until well combined. Spoon into the dish, pressing evenly and firmly over the base and side. Refrigerate.
2 Scrape the seeds from the vanilla bean into a saucepan. Add the pod, milk, cream and sugar and stir over medium heat until the sugar dissolves.
3 Whisk the egg yolks in a small bowl and slowly whisk in about 1/2 cup (125 ml) of the warm cream mixture. Return this mixture to the saucepan and cook over low heat, stirring constantly, for 10 minutes, or until the custard thickens and coats the back of a spoon. Strain into a bowl and refrigerate for 20 minutes.
4 Pour the mixture into a shallow metal tray and freeze for 1 1/2 hours until frozen around the edges. Transfer to a large bowl or food processor, beat until smooth, then pour back into the tray and return to the freezer. Repeat this three times. For the final freezing, pour the mixture into the pie dish and cover with baking paper.
5 To make the caramel, place the sugar and 1 tablespoon water in a small saucepan and stir over low heat

until the sugar has dissolved, brushing down the side of the pan with a clean pastry brush dipped in water if any crystals appear. Increase the heat, bring to the boil and cook, without stirring, until pale caramel. Remove from the heat and gradually add the cream, butter and 1 tablespoon of water. Return to the heat and bring

to the boil, stirring well. Remove and cool for 20 minutes. When slightly warm, spoon the caramel over the pie. Freeze until hard. Serve with any remaining caramel.

NUTRITION PER SERVE (8)
Protein 6.5 g; Fat 59 g; Carbohydrate 59.5 g; Dietary Fibre 0.5 g; Cholesterol 294.5 mg; 3255 kJ (780 cal)

Stir the custard mixture until it thickens and coats the back of a spoon.

Spread the ice cream over the biscuit mixture in the pie dish.

FRUIT MINCE PIES

Preparation time: 40 minutes
    + 40 minutes refrigeration
Cooking time: 25 minutes
Makes 24

Pastry
2 cups (250 g) plain flour
1/2 teaspoon ground cinnamon
125 g unsalted butter, chilled
    and cubed
1 teaspoon finely grated orange rind
1/4 cup (30 g) icing sugar, sifted
1 egg yolk
3–4 tablespoons iced water

Filling
1/3 cup (55 g) raisins, chopped
1/3 cup (60 g) soft brown sugar
1/4 cup (40 g) sultanas
1/4 cup (45 g) mixed peel
1 tablespoon currants
1 tablespoon chopped blanched
    almonds
1 small Granny Smith apple, grated
1 teaspoon lemon juice
1 teaspoon finely grated lemon rind
1 teaspoon finely grated orange rind
1/2 teaspoon mixed spice
1/4 teaspoon grated fresh ginger
pinch of ground nutmeg
25 g unsalted butter, melted
1 tablespoon brandy

1 Sift the flour, cinnamon and
1/4 teaspoon salt into a large bowl.
Add the butter and rub it into the
flour with your fingertips until it
resembles fine breadcrumbs. Stir in
the orange rind and icing sugar and
mix. Make a well in the centre and
add the egg yolk and 3–4 tablespoons
water. Mix with a flat-bladed knife,
using a cutting action, until the
mixture comes together in beads,
adding more water if necessary.
Gather together and lift out onto a
lightly floured work surface and press
together into a ball. Flatten slightly
into a disc, cover in plastic wrap
and refrigerate for 20 minutes.
2 Combine all the filling ingredients
in a bowl.
3 Preheat the oven to moderate
180°C (350°F/Gas 4). Grease two
12-hole shallow patty tins. Roll out
two-thirds of the pastry between two
sheets of baking paper until about
3 mm thick. Use a biscuit cutter to
cut out 24 x 7.5 cm rounds and place
them in the patty tins.
4 Divide the filling among the patty
cases. Roll out the remaining pastry
and cut out 12 rounds with a 7 cm
cutter. Using a 2.5 cm star cutter, cut
a star from the centre of each and use
this small piece to top 12 of the pies.
Use the outside part to top the other
12, pressing the edges together to
seal. Refrigerate for 20 minutes.
5 Bake for 25 minutes, or until the
pastry is golden. Leave in the tins for
5 minutes, then carefully lift out onto
a wire rack to cool. Dust with icing
sugar if you wish, then serve.

NUTRITION PER PIE
Protein 1.5 g; Fat 6 g; Carbohydrate
16.5 g; Dietary Fibre 1 g; Cholesterol
23 mg; 535 kJ (130 cal)

COOK'S FILE
Note: Any extra fruit mince can be
stored in a sterilised jar in a cool, dark
place for up to 3 months.

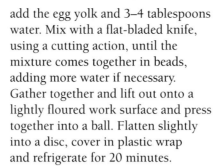

Use the fine side of the grater to grate the rind from the orange.

Stir the orange rind and icing sugar into the butter and flour mixture.

Mix the pastry using a cutting action until the mixture comes together in beads.

Carefully spoon the fruit mince mixture into the patty tins.

Cut a star shape from the centre of 12 of the pastry circles.

Top 12 of the pies with stars and the rest with the outside parts.

BLACKBERRY PIE

Preparation time: 20 minutes
 + 30 minutes refrigeration
Cooking time: 40 minutes
Serves 6

500 g home-made or bought sweet
 shortcrust pastry (see page 7)
500 g blackberries
2/3 cup (160 g) caster sugar
2 tablespoons cornflour
milk, to brush
1 egg, lightly beaten
caster sugar, extra,
 to sprinkle

1 Preheat the oven to moderately hot 200°C (400°F/Gas 6). Grease a 26 cm (top) 20.5 cm (base) 4.5 cm (deep) ceramic pie dish. Roll out two-thirds of the pastry between two sheets of baking paper until large enough to line the base and side of the pie dish. Remove the top paper, invert the pastry into the dish and press firmly into place.
2 Toss the blackberries (if frozen, thaw and drain well), sugar and cornflour together in a bowl until well mixed, then transfer to the pie dish. Roll out the remaining pastry between two sheets of baking paper until large enough to cover the pie.

Moisten the rim of the pie base with milk and press the pastry lid firmly into place. Trim and crimp the edges. Brush with egg and sprinkle with the extra sugar. Pierce the top of the pie with a knife.
3 Bake on the bottom shelf of the oven for 10 minutes. Reduce the oven to moderate 180°C (350°F/ Gas 4) and move the pie to the centre shelf. Bake for another 30 minutes, or until golden on top. Cool before serving with cream or ice cream.

NUTRITION PER SERVE
Protein 8.5 g; Fat 20 g; Carbohydrate 74.5 g; Dietary Fibre 7 g; Cholesterol 87 mg; 2120 kJ (505 cal)

Press the pastry into the pie dish, leaving any excess overhanging the edges.

Spoon the blackberry filling into the pastry-lined pie dish.

After brushing the lid with beaten egg, sprinkle it with caster sugar.

SHAKER LEMON PIE

Preparation time: 20 minutes
  + 20 minutes refrigeration
Cooking time: 50 minutes
Serves 6–8

2 lemons
½ cup (60 g) plain flour
2 cups (500 g) caster sugar
40 g unsalted butter, melted
4 eggs, lightly beaten
1 egg, extra, lightly beaten
icing sugar, for dusting
cream, for serving (optional)

Pastry

3 cups (375 g) plain flour
185 g unsalted butter, chilled
  and cubed
2 tablespoons caster sugar
4–5 tablespoons iced water

1 Finely grate 1 lemon to give
2 teaspoons of rind. Place this in
a large bowl. Cut the pith off both
lemons and discard. Thinly slice the
lemon flesh, discarding the seeds.
2 Sift the flour into the bowl with
the rind, then stir in the sugar and
a pinch of salt. Add the butter and
most of the egg and stir until smooth.
Gently fold in the lemon slices.
3 Preheat the oven to moderately
hot 200°C (400°F/Gas 6) and heat
a baking tray. Grease a 25 cm (top)
20 cm (base) 4 cm (deep) pie dish.
4 To make the pastry, sift the flour
and ¼ teaspoon salt into a large bowl
and rub in the butter with your
fingertips until the mixture resembles
fine breadcrumbs. Mix in the sugar.
Make a well, add almost all the water
and mix with a flat-bladed knife, using
a cutting action, until the mixture
comes together in beads, adding more
water if necessary. Gather together
and lift onto a lightly floured work
surface. Press into a ball and flatten
slightly into a disc. Wrap in plastic
wrap and refrigerate for 20 minutes.
5 Roll out two-thirds of the pastry to
a size large enough to fit the base and
side of the dish. Line the dish. Spoon
the filling into the pastry shell,

levelling the surface. Roll out the
remaining pastry until large enough
to cover the pie. Using a sharp knife,
cut out three small triangles in a row
across the centre of the lid. Brush the
rim of the pastry base with beaten
egg, then press the lid in place. Trim
off any excess. Scallop the edges with
your fingers, then go around the open
scallops and mark with the tines of a
narrow fork. Brush the top with egg.
6 Bake on the hot tray for 20 minutes.

*Use a small sharp knife to remove all of the
skin and pith from the lemons.*

Reduce the temperature to moderate
180°C (350°F/Gas 4), cover the pie
with foil and bake for 30 minutes, or
until the filling is set and the pastry
golden. Cool before serving. To serve,
place parallel strips of paper 2.5 cm
apart on the crust. Dust with icing
sugar, then carefully pull off the paper.

NUTRITION PER SERVE (8)
Protein 9 g; Fat 26 g; Carbohydrate
106.5 g; Dietary Fibre 2.5 g; Cholesterol
161 mg; 2880 kJ (690 cal)

*Gently fold the lemon slices into the butter
and egg mixture.*

FREEFORM BLUEBERRY PIE

Preparation time: 30 minutes
+ 20 minutes refrigeration
Cooking time: 30 minutes
Serves 6–8

Pastry

1¹/2 cups (185 g) plain flour
100 g unsalted butter, chilled and
  cubed
2 teaspoons grated orange rind
1 tablespoon caster sugar
2–3 tablespoons iced water

¹/3 cup (40 g) crushed amaretti
  biscuits or almond bread
¹/2 cup (60 g) plain flour
1 teaspoon ground cinnamon
¹/3 cup (90 g) caster sugar
500 g fresh blueberries
milk, for brushing
2 tablespoons blueberry jam
icing sugar, for dusting

1 Sift the flour into a large bowl and rub in the butter with your fingertips until the mixture resembles fine breadcrumbs. Stir in the orange rind and sugar. Make a well, add almost all the water and mix with a flat-bladed knife, using a cutting action, until the mixture comes together in beads. Add more water, a little at a time, if necessary to bring the dough together. Gather together and lift out onto a lightly floured surface. Press together into a ball and flatten it slightly into a disc. Wrap in plastic wrap and refrigerate for 20 minutes.
2 Preheat the oven to moderately hot 200°C (400°F/Gas 6). Combine the crushed biscuits, flour, cinnamon and 1¹/2 tablespoons sugar. Roll the pastry out to a 36 cm circle and sprinkle with the biscuit mixture, leaving a 4 cm border. Arrange the blueberries evenly over the crushed biscuits, then bring up the edges of the pie to form a freeform crust.
3 Brush the sides of the pie with the milk. Sprinkle with the remaining sugar and bake for 30 minutes, or until the sides are crisp and brown.
4 Warm the jam in a saucepan over low heat and brush over the berries. Allow the pie to cool to room temperature, then dust the pastry crust with sifted icing sugar.

NUTRITION PER SERVE (8)
Protein 4 g; Fat 12.5 g; Carbohydrate 50.5 g; Dietary Fibre 3 g; Cholesterol 32.5 mg; 1370 kJ (325 cal)

Sprinkle the crushed biscuit mixture over the pastry circle.

Arrange the blueberries over the biscuit mixture, then bring up the edges of the pie.

Brush the blueberries with the warmed blueberry jam to glaze.

LEMON MERINGUE PIE

Preparation time: 30 minutes
 + 20 minutes refrigeration
Cooking time: 50 minutes
Serves 4–6

375 g home-made or bought sweet
   shortcrust pastry (see page 7)
1/4 cup (30 g) plain flour
1/4 cup (30 g) cornflour
1 cup (250 g) caster sugar
3/4 cup (185 ml) lemon juice
1 tablespoon grated lemon rind
50 g unsalted butter, chopped
6 egg yolks

Meringue
6 egg whites
1 1/3 cups (340 g) caster sugar
pinch of cream of tartar

1 Lightly grease a 25 cm (top) 18 cm (base) 3 cm (deep) pie plate. Roll the pastry out between two sheets of baking paper into a 30 cm circle. Remove the top sheet of baking paper and invert the pastry into the pie plate. Trim the edges.

2 Re-roll the pastry trimmings and cut into three 10 x 2 cm strips. Brush the pie rim with water, place the pastry strips around the top of the pastry rim and use your fingers to make a decorative edge. Prick all over the base with a fork. Cover and refrigerate for 20 minutes. Preheat the oven to moderate 180°C (350°F/Gas 4).

3 Line the pastry with a sheet of baking paper that is large enough to cover the base and side of the pie plate, then pour in some baking beads or (uncooked) rice. Bake for 15 minutes, then remove the paper and beads and return to the oven for 15–20 minutes, or until the base is dry. Cool. Increase the oven to moderately hot 200°C (400°F/Gas 6).

4 To make the lemon filling, place the flours, sugar, lemon juice and rind in a saucepan. Gradually add 1 1/4 cups (315 ml) water and whisk over medium heat until smooth. Cook, stirring constantly for another 2 minutes, or until thickened. Remove from the heat and vigorously whisk in the butter and egg yolks. Return to low heat and stir constantly, for

2 minutes, or until very thick.

5 To make the meringue, beat the egg whites, sugar and cream of tartar in a clean, dry bowl, with electric beaters, for 10 minutes, or until thick and glossy.

6 Spread the lemon filling into the cooled pastry base, then spread the meringue over the top, piling high in the centre and making peaks with a knife. Bake for 8–10 minutes, or until lightly browned.

NUTRITION PER SERVE (6)
Protein 10.5 g; Fat 27.5 g; Carbohydrate 133 g; Dietary Fibre 1.5 g; Cholesterol 217 mg; 3385 kJ (810 cal)

Create peaks in the meringue with a flat-bladed knife.

DEEP-DISH APPLE PIE

Preparation time: 40 minutes
   + 20 minutes refrigeration
Cooking time: 50 minutes
Serves 6–8

Pastry
2 teaspoons semolina
1½ cups (185 g) plain flour
½ cup (60 g) self-raising flour
125 g unsalted butter, chilled
   and cubed
¼ cup (60 g) caster sugar
1 egg
3–4 tablespoons iced water

875 g apples, peeled, cored, halved
   and thinly sliced
¼ cup (60 g) caster sugar
½ teaspoon ground cinnamon
¼ teaspoon ground mixed spice
1 egg, separated
demerara sugar, to sprinkle

1 Grease a deep 24 cm (top) 19 cm (base) 5 cm (deep) pie dish, then sprinkle it with semolina. Sift the flours and ¼ teaspoon salt into a large bowl. Rub in the butter with your fingertips until the mixture resembles fine breadcrumbs. Mix in the sugar. Make a well in the centre, add the egg and most of the water and mix with a flat-bladed knife, using a cutting action, until the mixture comes together in beads, adding a little more water if necessary.

2 Gather the dough together and lift out onto a lightly floured work surface. Bring the dough together into a smooth ball, then flatten slightly into a disc, cover with plastic wrap and refrigerate for 20 minutes. Preheat the oven to moderately hot 200°C (400°F/Gas 6).

3 Meanwhile, combine the apple, sugar and spices in a large bowl.

4 Roll out the dough between two sheets of baking paper to a rough-edged 40 cm circle. Remove the top paper and place the pastry in the dish, leaving the edges overhanging. Brush the base with egg yolk. Pile the apple filling in the centre.

5 Bring the pastry edges up and over the filling, leaving a 4 cm gap in the centre. Tuck and fold the pastry as necessary. Brush the pastry with egg white and sprinkle with the demerara sugar. Bake for 20 minutes, then reduce the heat to moderate 180°C (350°F/Gas 4) and bake for another 30 minutes, or until the pastry is crisp and golden. Cover with foil if it is browning too much. Serve hot or at room temperature.

NUTRITION PER SERVE (8)
Protein 5.5 g; Fat 1.5 g; Carbohydrate 51 g; Dietary Fibre 3.5 g; Cholesterol 84.5 mg; 1470 kJ (350 cal)

Peel the apples, remove the cores, cut each in half, then thinly slice.

Brush the pastry with egg white and sprinkle with the demerara sugar.

ALMOND PIES

Preparation time: 20 minutes
Cooking time: 25 minutes
Makes 8

50 g flaked almonds
125 g unsalted butter, softened
1 cup (125 g) icing sugar
125 g ground almonds
¼ cup (30 g) plain flour
2 eggs
1 tablespoon rum or brandy
½ teaspoon vanilla essence
4 sheets frozen ready-made
   puff pastry, thawed

1 egg, lightly beaten
sugar, to sprinkle
icing sugar, for dusting

1 Preheat the oven to moderately hot 200°C (400°F/Gas 6). Bake the flaked almonds on a baking tray for 2–3 minutes, or until just golden. Remove and return the tray to the oven to keep it hot.
2 Beat together the butter, icing sugar, ground almonds, flour, eggs, rum and vanilla with electric beaters for 2–3 minutes, or until smooth and combined. Fold in the flaked almonds.
3 Cut out eight 10 cm rounds and eight 11 cm rounds from the puff

pastry. Spread the smaller rounds with equal amounts of filling, leaving a 1 cm border. Brush the borders with beaten egg and cover with the tops. Seal the edges with a fork and, if you wish, decorate the tops with shapes cut from pastry scraps. Pierce with a fork to allow steam to escape. Brush with egg and sprinkle with sugar. Bake on the hot tray for 15–20 minutes, or until the pastry is puffed and golden. Dust with icing sugar.

NUTRITION PER PIE
Protein 12 g; Fat 46 g; Carbohydrate 49.5 g; Dietary Fibre 3 g; Cholesterol 128 mg; 2750 kJ (655 cal)

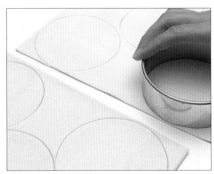

Use a biscuit cutter to cut out the rounds of puff pastry.

Divide the filling among the eight puff pastry bases.

Seal the top pastry to the bottom by crimping the edges with a fork.

Creams and custards

A home-made pie married with a delicious creamy sauce or custard is a special treat you'll feel proud to serve to your family and friends. The recipes below are enough to serve about four to six people.

SYLLABUB

Stir together ¹/₂ cup (125 ml) Champagne or medium–dry white wine, 1 tablespoon brandy, 1 teaspoon finely grated lemon peel and ¹/₄ cup (60 g) caster sugar in a bowl. Set aside for 1 hour, stirring occasionally to help dissolve the sugar. Add 1¹/₄ cups (315 ml) chilled thick cream and gently whip until soft peaks are formed. Serve immediately or chill until ready to serve. The syllabub will keep refrigerated for two days.

ZABAGLIONE

Place 4 egg yolks and ¹/₄ cup (60 g) caster sugar into a large heatproof bowl. Using electric beaters, beat the eggs and sugar for 1–2 minutes, or until the mixture is light and creamy. Stand the bowl over a saucepan of barely simmering water, add 2 tablespoons Cointreau and continue beating for 5–6 minutes, or until the mixture is thick, light and foamy. Serve immediately, as it will separate if left standing.

Note: Zabaglione is known as sabayon in France and is traditionally made in a copper bowl. For this luxurious sauce, you can use any flavour of liqueur, choosing one that will complement the flavour of the filling in the pie the zabaglione is to be served with.

Clockwise from back: Syllabub; Zabaglione; English custard; Brandy cream sauce; Yoghurt cream

ENGLISH CUSTARD

Using a wire whisk or hand beater, beat 3 egg yolks and 2 tablespoons sugar in a bowl for about 3 minutes, or until the mixture is very light and creamy. Place 1½ cups (375 ml) milk and a vanilla bean that has been split and scraped into a small saucepan and stir over low heat until the mixture comes to the boil. Remove the vanilla bean and pour slowly onto the egg mixture, whisking constantly. Return to the pan and stir with a wooden spoon over very low heat for about 5 minutes, or until the custard thickens. Do not allow the mixture to boil or it will curdle. Test the consistency by dipping the spoon into the custard and drawing your finger in a line down the back of the spoon—it should leave a clean line. Remove from the heat. English custard may be served warm or cool. Cover with plastic wrap if storing in the refrigerator.

Note: As a variation you can stir 1–2 tablespoons of your favourite liqueur through the custard.

BRANDY CREAM SAUCE

Beat 2 egg yolks and ⅓ cup (90 g) caster sugar until thick and pale and all the sugar has dissolved. Stir in ⅓ cup (80 ml) brandy and fold in 1 cup (250 ml) cream. Beat 2 egg whites in a clean, dry bowl until soft peaks form. Fold into the sauce and serve immediately.

YOGHURT CREAM

Beat 1 cup (250 ml) cream in a small bowl until it forms soft peaks. Gently fold the cream into 1 cup (250 g) natural yoghurt. Pour the cream mixture into a 3 cup (750 ml) serving dish that is about 5 cm deep. Smooth the top of the mixture and sprinkle with ¼ cup (45 g) soft brown sugar. The brown sugar should form an even layer and completely cover the top of the cream mixture. Refrigerate the mixture for at least 2 hours to allow the sugar to caramelise on the top.

PEACH PIE

Preparation time: 35 minutes
   + 20 minutes refrigeration
Cooking time: 55 minutes
Serves 6

500 g home-made or bought sweet
   shortcrust pastry (see page 6)
2 x 825 g cans peach slices,
   well-drained
½ cup (125 g) caster sugar
¼ cup (30 g) cornflour
¼ teaspoon almond essence
20 g unsalted butter, chopped
1 tablespoon milk
1 egg, lightly beaten
caster sugar, to sprinkle

1 Roll out two-thirds of the dough
between two sheets of baking paper
until large enough to line a 23 cm
(top) 18 cm (base) 3 cm (deep) pie
tin. Remove the top sheet of paper
and invert the pastry into the tin.
Use a small ball of pastry to help
press the pastry into the tin, allowing
any excess to hang over. Use a sharp
knife to trim any extra pastry.
Refrigerate for 20 minutes.
2 Preheat the oven to moderately
hot 200°C (400°F/Gas 6). Line the
pastry with crumpled baking paper to
cover the base and side and pour in
baking beads or (uncooked) rice. Bake
for 10 minutes, remove the paper and
beads and return to the oven for
5 minutes, until the base is dry and
lightly coloured. Allow to cool.
3 Combine the peaches, caster sugar,
cornflour and almond essence in a
bowl. Mix, then spoon into the
cooled pastry shell. Dot with butter
and moisten the edges with milk.

4 Roll out the remaining dough to a
25 cm square. Using a fluted pastry
cutter, cut the pastry into ten strips
2.5 cm wide. Lay the strips in a
lattice pattern over the filling. Press
firmly on the edges and trim. Brush
the lattice with egg and sprinkle with
sugar. Bake for 10 minutes, reduce
the heat to moderate 180°C (350°F/
Gas 4) and bake for 30 minutes, or
until the top is golden. Cool before
serving. Delicious with ice cream.

NUTRITION PER SERVE
Protein 7 g; Fat 25 g; Carbohydrate
69.5 g; Dietary Fibre 3 g; Cholesterol
62 mg; 2195 kJ (525 cal)

*Combine the peaches with the caster sugar,
cornflour and almond essence.*

*Lay the pastry strips in a lattice pattern
over the filling.*

BANANA CREAM PIE

Preparation time: 25 minutes
+ 20 minutes refrigeration
+ cooling
Cooking time: 30 minutes
Serves 6–8

375 g home-made or bought
   shortcrust pastry (see page 6)
80 g dark chocolate melts
4 egg yolks
½ cup (125 g) caster sugar
½ teaspoon vanilla essence
2 tablespoons custard powder
2 cups (500 ml) milk
40 g unsalted butter, softened
1 teaspoon brandy or rum
3 large ripe bananas, plus extra,
   to decorate
50 g dark chocolate, grated or
   shaved, to decorate

1 Roll out the pastry between two sheets of baking paper until large enough to line a 23 cm (top) 18 cm (base) 3 cm (deep) pie tin. Remove the top sheet of paper and invert the pastry into the tin. Use a small ball of pastry to help press the pastry into the tin, allowing any excess to hang over the sides. Use a small sharp knife to trim away any extra pastry. Refrigerate for 20 minutes.

2 Preheat the oven to moderately hot 190°C (375°F/Gas 5). Line the pastry with crumpled baking paper to cover the base and side of the tin and pour in baking beads or (uncooked) rice. Bake for 10 minutes, remove the paper and beads and return to the oven for 10–12 minutes, until the base is dry, lightly coloured and cooked through.

3 While the pastry base is still hot, place the chocolate melts in the shell. Leave for 5 minutes to allow the chocolate to melt, then spread the chocolate over the base crust with the back of a spoon or a small palette knife. Allow to cool a little.

4 To make the filling, place the egg yolks, sugar, vanilla and custard powder in a bowl and beat with electric beaters for 2–3 minutes, or

until pale and thick. Bring the milk to the boil in a small saucepan over medium heat. When the milk begins to boil, remove from the heat and gradually pour into the egg and sugar mixture, stirring well. Return the mixture to the saucepan and bring to the boil over medium heat, stirring well. Cook for 2 minutes, or until the custard has thickened. Remove from the heat and stir in the butter and

brandy. Set aside to cool completely.
5 Slice the bananas into 3–4 mm slices, arrange over the chocolate, then pour the custard over the top. Refrigerate until ready to serve. Decorate with extra banana slices and the grated chocolate.

NUTRITION PER SERVE (8)
Protein 8 g; Fat 25.5 g; Carbohydrate 59.5 g; Dietary Fibre 2 g; Cholesterol 123.5 mg; 2060 kJ (490 cal)

Beat the egg and sugar mixture until it is pale and thick.

Pour the custard into the pie shell over the banana slices.

OLD-FASHIONED APPLE PIE

Preparation time: 40 minutes
+ 40 minutes refrigeration + cooling
Cooking time: 55 minutes
Serves 8

Pastry
2 cups (250 g) self-raising flour
2/3 cup (85 g) cornflour
180 g unsalted butter, chilled, cubed
1/3 cup (90 g) caster sugar
1 egg, lightly beaten

40 g unsalted butter
6 green apples, peeled, cored
    and thinly sliced
1 tablespoon lemon juice
3/4 cup (140 g) soft brown sugar
1 teaspoon ground nutmeg
2 tablespoons plain flour
1/4 cup (25 g) ground almonds
milk, to brush
sugar, to sprinkle

1 Lightly grease a 1 litre, 20 cm metal pie dish. Sift the flour and cornflour into a large bowl and rub in the butter with your fingertips until the mixture resembles fine breadcrumbs. Stir in the sugar and a pinch of salt. Make a well in the centre, add the egg and mix with a knife, using a cutting action, until the mixture comes together in beads. **2** Gather the dough together, turn out onto a lightly floured work surface and press together until smooth. Press into a disc, cover with plastic wrap and refrigerate for 20 minutes. **3** Roll out two-thirds of the dough between two sheets of baking paper until large enough to line the base and side of the dish. Remove the top paper and invert the pastry into the dish, allowing any excess to hang over the sides. Roll the remaining pastry between the baking paper until large enough to cover the dish. Cover and refrigerate both pastry rounds for 20 minutes. Preheat the oven to moderately hot 200°C (400°F/Gas 6) and heat a baking tray in the oven. **4** To make the filling, melt the butter in a large frying pan, add the apple and toss. Stir in the lemon juice, brown sugar and nutmeg and cook for 5–10 minutes, or until tender. Combine the flour with 1/4 cup (60 ml) water, then add to the mixture. Add the almonds, bring to the boil and cook, stirring, for 2–3 minutes, or until thickened. Pour into a bowl and leave to cool. **5** Put the apple in the pastry case. Cover with pastry and press lightly onto the rim. Trim the edges and pinch together to seal. Decorate with leftover cut-outs. Using a small, sharp knife, prick the top all over. Brush lightly with milk and sprinkle with sugar. Place on the hot tray and bake for 40 minutes, or until golden brown. Cool slightly before serving.

NUTRITION PER SERVE
Protein 5.5 g; Fat 26 g; Carbohydrate 74.5 g; Dietary Fibre 4 g; Cholesterol 92 mg; 2280 kJ (545 cal)

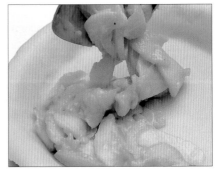

Spoon the apple mixture into the pastry-lined pie dish.

PEAR AND APPLE CRUMBLE PIE

Preparation time: 20 minutes
    + 20 minutes refrigeration + cooling
Cooking time: 1 hour 10 minutes
Serves 6–8

375 g home-made or bought
    shortcrust pastry (see page 6)
3 pears
4 Granny Smith apples
1/4 cup (60 g) caster sugar
2 teaspoons grated orange rind
90 g raisins
3/4 cup (90 g) plain flour
1/2 cup (95 g) soft brown sugar
1/2 teaspoon ground ginger
90 g unsalted butter

1 Roll the pastry between two sheets of baking paper until large enough to cover the base and side of a 23 cm (top) 18 cm (base) 3 cm (deep) pie dish. Remove the top baking paper and invert the pastry into the dish. Trim the excess. Cover with plastic wrap and refrigerate for 20 minutes.

2 Meanwhile, peel, core and slice the pears and apples and place in a large saucepan. Add the sugar, orange rind and 2 tablespoons water and cook over low heat, stirring occasionally for 20 minutes, or until the fruit is tender but still holding its shape. Remove from the heat, add the raisins and a pinch of salt, mix and set aside to cool completely before spooning into the pastry case.

3 Preheat the oven to moderately hot 200°C (400°F/Gas 6) and preheat a baking tray. To make the topping, combine the flour, brown sugar and ginger in a bowl and rub in the butter

with your fingertips until the mixture resembles coarse breadcrumbs. Sprinkle on top of the fruit.

4 Place the pie dish on the hot baking tray, bake for 10 minutes, then reduce the oven temperature to moderate 180°C (350°F/Gas 4) and cook the pie for 40 minutes, or until nicely browned. Cover the pie with foil halfway through if the top is browning too quickly. Serve warm with cream.

NUTRITION PER SERVE (8)
Protein 5 g; Fat 21.5 g; Carbohydrate 72 g; Dietary Fibre 4.5 g; Cholesterol 41.5 mg; 2055 kJ (490 cal)

Cook the pear and apple pieces, stirring occasionally, until tender.

Sprinkle the crumble mixture over the pear and apple filling.

PEAR AND PECAN PIE

Preparation time: 25 minutes
+ 40 minutes refrigeration + cooling
Cooking time: 50 minutes
Serves 6

Pastry

1½ cups (185 g) plain flour
75 g unsalted butter, chilled and cubed
50 g Copha (white vegetable shortening), chilled and cubed
1 teaspoon caster sugar
2–3 tablespoons iced water

40 g unsalted butter
½ cup (175 g) golden syrup
2 tablespoons cornflour
¼ teaspoon ground ginger
½ teaspoon grated lemon rind
½ teaspoon mixed spice
4 pears, peeled, cored and thinly sliced
1 cup (100 g) pecans, chopped
1 tablespoon caster sugar
1 tablespoon ground pecans
1 tablespoon sugar
1 egg, lightly beaten

1 To make the pastry, sift the flour and ¼ teaspoon salt into a large bowl and rub in the butter and Copha with your fingertips until the mixture resembles fine breadcrumbs. Mix in the sugar. Make a well, add almost all the water and mix with a flat-bladed knife, using a cutting action, until the mixture comes together in beads, adding more water if necessary.
2 Gather the dough together and lift onto a lightly floured work surface. Press into a ball and flatten slightly into a disc. Cover in plastic wrap and refrigerate for 20 minutes.
3 Preheat the oven to moderately hot 200°C (400°F/Gas 6) and heat a baking tray. Grease a 23 cm (top) 18 cm (base) x 3 cm (deep) pie dish. Roll out two-thirds of the pastry between two sheets of baking paper until large enough to cover the base and side of the dish. Remove the top paper and invert the pastry into the pie dish. Cover and refrigerate for 20 minutes.
4 For the filling, heat the butter and golden syrup in a saucepan over medium heat for 2 minutes. Add the cornflour, ginger, rind and mixed spice and stir until smooth. Add the pears, then stir in half the chopped pecans and cook for 5 minutes, or until the pear is tender. Cool completely.
5 Combine the caster sugar and remaining chopped pecans and scatter over the pastry base. Add the filling.
6 Combine the ground pecans and sugar. Roll out the remaining pastry to form a pie lid. Brush with beaten egg. Cut long strips of thick paper 3 cm wide and place at 3 cm intervals on the lid. Scatter the nut and sugar mixture over the exposed pastry and roll lightly with the rolling pin to embed them. Lift off the paper, then position the lid on the pie, pinching the edges down to seal. Trim the rim.
7 Bake on the hot tray in the centre of the oven for 20 minutes. Reduce the temperature to moderate 180°C (350°F/Gas 4), cover the top with foil and bake for another 20 minutes. Cool in the tin. Serve warm or cold.

NUTRITION PER SERVE
Protein 6.5 g; Fat 33.5 g; Carbohydrate 69 g; Dietary Fibre 5 g; Cholesterol 61.5 mg; 2485 kJ (595 cal)

Peel the pears, remove the cores, and cut them into thin slices.

Add the cornflour, ginger, lemon rind and mixed spice and stir until smooth.

Spoon the pear mixture over the base of the pastry shell.

Scatter the nut and sugar mixture over the exposed stripes.

Carefully remove the paper strips from the pastry sheet.

Position the lid on the pie and trim the edges neatly.

CHOCOLATE AND PEANUT BUTTER PIE

Preparation time: 30 minutes
  + 4 hours 15 minutes refrigeration
Cooking time: 5 minutes
Serves 10–12

200 g chocolate biscuits with cream
  centre, crushed
50 g unsalted butter, melted
1 cup (250 g) cream cheese
2/3 cup (85 g) icing sugar, sifted
1/2 cup (125 g) smooth peanut butter
1 teaspoon vanilla essence
300 ml cream, whipped to firm peaks
1/4 cup (60 ml) cream, extra
3 teaspoons unsalted butter, extra
100 g dark chocolate, grated
honey-roasted peanuts, to garnish

1 Combine the chocolate biscuit crumbs with the melted butter and press into the base and side of a deep 23 cm (top) 18 cm (base) 3 cm (deep) pie dish and refrigerate for 15 minutes, or until firm.
2 Meanwhile, place the cream cheese and icing sugar in a bowl and beat with electric beaters until smooth. Add the peanut butter and vanilla and beat together well. Stir in a third of the whipped cream until the mixture is smooth, then very gently fold in the remaining whipped cream.
3 Pour two-thirds of the mixture into the pie shell and smooth the top—the remaining mixture is used for the garnish. Refrigerate the pie and the remaining mixture for 2 hours, or until firm.
4 When the pie is firm, place the extra cream and butter in a small saucepan and stir over medium heat until the butter is melted and the cream just comes to a simmer. Remove from the heat and add the grated chocolate, stirring until the chocolate is melted and the mixture is smooth and silky. Allow to cool to room temperature, then pour over the top of the pie, smoothing if necessary with a spatula dipped in hot water. Refrigerate for another 2 hours, or until the topping is firm. Remove the extra filling from the refrigerator about 30 minutes before you are ready to serve.
5 To garnish, fill a piping bag with the softened peanut butter mixture and pipe rosettes or use two small spoons to dollop around the edges of the pie. Top each rosette or dollop with a honey-roasted peanut. Serve in thin wedges as this pie is very rich.

NUTRITION PER SERVE (12)
Protein 6.5 g; Fat 35 g; Carbohydrate 25 g; Dietary Fibre 1.5 g; Cholesterol 75.5 mg; 1820 kJ (435 cal)

Gently fold the whipped cream into the peanut butter mixture.

Pour the cooled chocolate over the top of the pie and smooth with a spatula.

WALNUT PIE WITH CARAMEL SAUCE

Preparation time: 40 minutes
  + refrigeration + cooling
Cooking time: 40 minutes
Serves 6–8

Pastry
2 cups (250 g) plain flour
180 g unsalted butter, chilled, cubed
1/3 cup (40 g) icing sugar
1 egg yolk
3–4 tablespoons iced water

Filling
2 eggs
210 g caster sugar
150 g walnuts, finely chopped

Caramel sauce
40 g unsalted butter
1 1/4 cups (230 g) soft brown sugar
2 teaspoons vanilla essence
200 ml cream

1 egg yolk, lightly beaten
icing sugar, to garnish
walnuts, to garnish

1 Sift the flour and 1/2 teaspoon salt into a large bowl and rub in the butter using your fingertips until the mixture resembles fine breadcrumbs. Mix in the icing sugar. Make a well, add the egg yolk and almost all the water and mix with a flat-bladed knife, using a cutting action, until the mixture comes together in beads.
2 Gather the dough together and lift onto a lightly floured work surface. Press together into a ball and flatten slightly into a disc. Cover in plastic wrap and refrigerate for 20 minutes.
3 Preheat the oven to moderate 180°C (350°F/Gas 4). Grease a fluted 36 x 11 cm pie tin. Place the eggs and sugar in a bowl and beat with a spoon or whisk for 2 minutes. Stir in the walnuts.
4 Divide the dough into two portions, one slightly larger than the other. Roll the larger portion out between two sheets of baking paper until large enough to line the base

and side of the pie tin. Line the pie tin. Refrigerate, covered in plastic wrap, while you roll out the remaining pastry to a size large enough to cover the top of the tin.
5 Pour the walnut filling into the pastry case, brush the rim with the egg yolk and position the lid in place, pressing the edges to seal. Trim the edge. Make a steam hole in the top. Brush with egg yolk and bake for 30–35 minutes. Leave to cool for

at least 1 hour (do not refrigerate).
6 To make the caramel sauce, place the butter, sugar, vanilla and cream in a saucepan and cook, stirring, for 5 minutes, or until thick. Dust the pie with icing sugar and sprinkle with walnuts. Drizzle with the caramel sauce.

NUTRITION PER SERVE (8)
Protein 9 g; Fat 49.5 g; Carbohydrate 83.5 g; Dietary Fibre 2.5 g; Cholesterol 193 mg; 3345 kJ (800 cal)

Pour the walnut filling into the pastry case and brush the rim with beaten egg yolk.

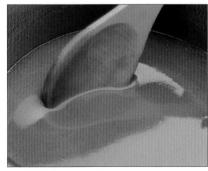
To make the caramel sauce, heat the butter, sugar, vanilla and cream and stir until thick.

QUINCE PIE WITH STICKY SYRUP

Preparation time: 50 minutes
+ 20 minutes refrigeration
Cooking time: 3 hours
Serves 6–8

2 cups (440 g) demerara sugar
1 vanilla bean, split in half
6 cardamom pods, bruised
2 star anise
1 cinnamon stick
2 kg quinces, peeled, cored and
    cut into large wedges

Pastry
100 g plain flour
100 g self-raising flour
100 g lard, chilled and grated
1–2 tablespoons iced water
2 tablespoons milk
1/4 teaspoon ground cinnamon
2 teaspoons caster sugar

1 Place the sugar, vanilla bean, cardamom, star anise and cinnamon in a stockpot or very large saucepan with 1 litre water, and stir over low heat until the sugar dissolves. Add the quinces and bring to the boil, then reduce the heat and simmer for 2 hours, or until orange and tender.
2 Remove the quinces with a slotted spoon and set aside. Strain the syrup into a bowl, then return it to the pan and boil for 10 minutes, or until reduced, thick and sticky.
3 Preheat the oven to 200°C (400°F/ Gas 6). Sift the flours and a little salt into a large bowl, add the lard and rub it into the flour with your fingertips until it resembles fine breadcrumbs. Make a well in the centre, add the water and mix with a flat-bladed knife, using a cutting action, until the mixture comes together in beads.
3 Gently gather the dough together and lift onto a lightly floured surface. Press together into a ball and flatten slightly into a disc. Cover in plastic wrap and refrigerate for 20 minutes.
4 Spoon the quince filling into a 26 cm (top) 21 cm (base) 3 cm (deep) pie plate and mix in 1/2 cup (125 ml) of the reserved syrup. Roll the dough out between two sheets of baking paper until large enough to cover the pie. Remove the top paper and invert the pastry onto the pie, allowing any excess to hang over, and pinch the edges to seal. Trim away any excess pastry. Cut steam holes in the top and decorate with pastry scraps. Brush the pastry with milk and sprinkle the combined cinnamon and sugar over the pie. Place the pie plate on a baking tray and bake for 35–40 minutes, or until crisp and golden. Warm the remaining syrup and serve with the pie.

NUTRITION PER SERVE (8)
Protein 3.5 g; Fat 13 g; Carbohydrate 66.5 g; Dietary Fibre 12 g; Cholesterol 12.5 mg; 1645 kJ (395 cal)

Pour the syrup over the quince filling in the pie plate.

KEY LIME PIE

Preparation time: 10 minutes
Cooking time: 40 minutes
Serves 6–8

375 g home-made or bought sweet
   shortcrust pastry (see page 7)
4 egg yolks
395 g can condensed milk
½ cup (125 ml) lime juice
2 teaspoons grated lime rind

1 Preheat the oven to moderate 180°C (350°F/Gas 4). Grease a 23 cm (top) 18 cm (base) 2 cm (deep) pie tin. Roll the dough out between two sheets of baking paper until it is large enough to fit into the pie tin. Remove the top sheet of paper and invert the pastry into the tin. Use a small ball of pastry to help press the pastry into the tin, allowing any excess to hang over the sides. Use a small sharp knife to trim away any extra pastry.
2 Line the pastry shell with a piece of crumpled baking paper that is large enough to cover the base and side of the tin and pour in some baking beads or (uncooked) rice. Bake for 10 minutes, remove the paper and beads and return the pastry to the oven for another 4–5 minutes, or until the base is dry. Leave the crust to cool.
3 Using electric beaters, beat the egg yolks, condensed milk, lime juice and rind in a large bowl for 2 minutes, or until well combined. Pour into the pie shell and smooth the surface. Bake for 20–25 minutes, or until set. Allow the pie to cool, then refrigerate for 2 hours, or until well chilled. Delicious served with whipped cream and can be garnished with lime slices and dusted with sifted icing sugar.

NUTRITION PER SERVE (8)
Protein 8.5 g; Fat 19 g; Carbohydrate 47 g; Dietary Fibre 1 g; Cholesterol 119.5 mg; 1615 kJ (385 cal)

COOK'S FILE
Note: If the pie looks like it is browning a little, don't cover it with foil because the foil will stick to the top.

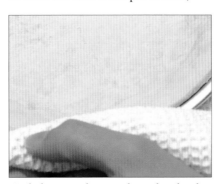

Cook the pastry base until it is dry, then let the crust cool.

Thoroughly mix all the filling ingredients together.

RAISIN PIE

Preparation time: 15 minutes
+ 20 minutes refrigeration
cooling
Cooking time: 1 hour
Serves 6–8

600 g home-made or bought sweet
shortcrust pastry (see page 7)
1/3 cup (80 ml) orange juice
2 tablespoons lemon juice
2 cups (320 g) raisins
3/4 cup (140 g) soft brown sugar
1/2 teaspoon mixed spice
1/4 cup (30 g) cornflour
1 teaspoon finely grated lemon rind
1 teaspoon finely grated orange rind
1 egg, lightly beaten
1 tablespoon sugar, to sprinkle

1 Preheat the oven to moderately hot 190°C (375°F/Gas 5). Place a baking tray in the oven to preheat. Grease a 23 cm (top) 18 cm (base) 3 cm (deep) pie tin.
2 Roll out two-thirds of the pastry between two sheets of baking paper to fit the base and side of the dish. Remove the top paper and invert the pastry into the tin. Use a small ball of pastry to help press the pastry into the tin, allowing any excess to hang over the sides. Use a small sharp knife to trim away any extra pastry. Chill the base and remaining pastry while you prepare the fruit.
3 Combine the citrus juices, raisins and 1 cup (250 ml) water in a small saucepan. Boil over high heat, stirring occasionally, for 2 minutes. Remove from the heat.
4 Mix the brown sugar, mixed spice and cornflour in a bowl. Add 1/2 cup (125 ml) water and mix to a smooth paste. Slowly stir into the raisin mixture and return the saucepan to the stove over high heat. Bring to the boil, stirring regularly, then reduce the heat and simmer, stirring occasionally, for 5 minutes, or until the mixture thickens and reduces slightly. Stir in the citrus rind and set aside to cool for 30 minutes.
5 Roll out the remaining pastry to cover the pie. Fill the base with the raisin mixture, brush the edges with beaten egg and cover with the pastry top, pinching the edges together and making a few small holes with a skewer. Decorate if you wish. Brush with egg, sprinkle with sugar and bake for 40–45 minutes, or until the pastry is golden. Serve warm, with custard if desired, or cold.

NUTRITION PER SERVE (8)
Protein 6 g; Fat 20 g; Carbohydrate 76 g; Dietary Fibre 3 g; Cholesterol 43.5 mg; 2095 kJ (500 cal)

Use a small ball of excess pastry to press the pastry into the tin.

PLUM PIE

Preparation time: 15 minutes
    + 20 minutes refrigeration
Cooking time: 55 minutes
Serves 6–8

600 g home-made or bought sweet
    shortcrust pastry (see page 7)
14 large plums, halved, stoned
    and roughly chopped,
    or 2 x 825 g tins plums, drained
1/2 cup (95 g) soft brown sugar
1 teaspoon grated lemon rind
1 teaspoon grated orange rind
30 g unsalted butter, softened
2 tablespoons plain flour

1/2 teaspoon ground cinnamon
1 egg, lightly beaten
caster sugar, for sprinkling

1 Preheat the oven to moderate 180°C (350°F/Gas 4). Lightly grease a 23 cm (top) 18 cm (base) 3 cm (deep) pie tin.
2 Roll out two thirds of the pastry between two sheets of baking paper to fit the base and side of the tin. Remove the top sheet of paper and invert the pastry into the tin. Use a small ball of pastry to press the pastry into the tin, allowing any excess to hang over the sides. Use a small sharp knife to trim away any extra pastry. Refrigerate the base

and remaining pastry for 20 minutes.
3 Combine the plums, brown sugar, citrus rind and butter in a large bowl. Sift the flour and cinnamon together over the plums and fold through. Place in the pie tin. Roll out the remaining pastry to cover the tin. Put in place and trim. Pinch the edges and make a 1 cm diameter hole in the centre. Brush with egg and bake for 50–55 minutes, or until the plums are tender and the pastry is golden. Sprinkle with caster sugar before serving.

NUTRITION PER SERVE (8)
Protein 6.5 g; Fat 23 g; Carbohydrate 54 g; Dietary Fibre 4.5 g; Cholesterol 53 mg; 1870 kJ (445 cal)

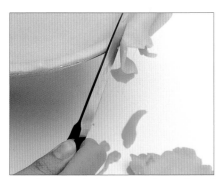
Line the tin with the pastry and trim the edges with a small sharp knife.

Fold the sifted flour and cinnamon through the plum mixture.

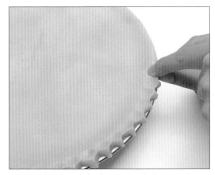
Cover the pie with the pastry lid, trim the edges and pinch to seal.

LIME AND BLUEBERRY PIE

Preparation time: 30 minutes
    + 20 minutes refrigeration
Cooking time: 55 minutes
Serves 6–8

375 g home-made or bought sweet
    shortcrust pastry (see page 7)
3 eggs
½ cup (125 g) caster sugar
¼ cup (60 ml) buttermilk
1 tablespoon lime juice
2 teaspoons grated lime rind
2 tablespoons custard powder
250 g blueberries
icing sugar, to dust

1 Roll out the pastry between two sheets of baking paper to line a 23 cm (top) 18 cm (base) 3 cm (deep) pie tin. Remove the top paper and invert the pastry into the tin. Use a small ball of pastry to press the pastry into the tin, allowing any excess to hang over, then trim. Refrigerate for 20 minutes.

2 Preheat the oven to moderately hot 200°C (400°F/Gas 6). Line the base and side of the pastry with crumpled baking paper and pour in baking beads or (uncooked) rice. Bake for 10 minutes, remove the paper and beads and bake for 4–5 minutes, or until the base is dry and lightly coloured. Cool slightly. Reduce the oven temperature to moderate 180°C (350°F/Gas 4).
3 To make the filling, beat the eggs and caster sugar in a bowl with electric beaters until the mixture is thick and pale. Add the buttermilk, lime juice and rind, and sifted

custard powder. Stir until combined, then spoon into the pastry shell. Bake for 15 minutes, then reduce the temperature to warm 160°C (315°F/Gas 2–3) and cook for another 20–25 minutes, or until the filling has coloured slightly and is set. Cool (the filling will sink while cooling), then top with the blueberries. Dust with sifted icing sugar and serve.

NUTRITION PER SERVE (8)
Protein 5.5 g; Fat 14 g; Carbohydrate 38.5 g; Dietary Fibre 1 g; Cholesterol 81.5 mg; 1240 kJ (295 cal)

Bake the pastry, then remove the paper and beads and bake for another 5 minutes.

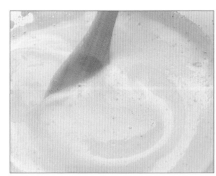

Stir the buttermilk, lime juice, rind and custard powder into the egg mixture.